To Dad
With many
wishes for a
happy birthday
Much Love,
Brian & Rob

WHAT'S THE MATTER WITH THE RED SOX?

What's the Matter with the Red Sox?

◆

by AL HIRSHBERG

DODD, MEAD & COMPANY
NEW YORK

ISBN: 0-396-06807-3
Library of Congress Catalog Card Number: 73-2133

Printed in the United States of America
by The Cornwall Press, Inc., Cornwall, N. Y.

To Margie,
who would have liked this one

Introduction

What's the matter with the Red Sox?

In Boston, in all of New England except southern Connecticut, in the Maritime Provinces—wherever baseball is discussed in these areas—this was first a plaintive cry, then a chronic complaint, and finally a way of life.

If this territory seems large, even for a major-league baseball team, it is; the Boston Red Sox *do* cover a lot of territory. Even Canada's own big-league club in Montreal has failed to take the Maritime Provinces out of the Red Sox orbit. Down Easters and their neighbors across the border are, as they have been almost since the turn of the century, among the ball club's most rabid fans.

The fortunes of the team have gone up and down like a yo-yo. Public interest in it, however, has not wavered. Good, bad, or indifferent, Red Sox teams have consistently been the hottest sports subject in the northeast, especially since the day in 1933 when a young multimillionaire named Tom Yawkey bought the franchise from a poor but proud syndicate headed by Bob Quinn. In the hearts of their fans, the ups of the Red Sox have brought ecstasy, the downs misery, and their failures in the face of success derision and sometimes cold anger.

Red Sox fans have been living and dying with their favorites for three-quarters of a century. Big-league baseball may fluctuate sharply elsewhere, but not in Boston. Give a losing Red Sox team a three-game winning streak, and the club's home, Fenway Park, will be mobbed for a week following. Give a Red Sox team a shot at the pennant, and Fenway Park, the most picturesque and one of the oldest and smallest baseball plants in either major league, will be mobbed for a year following. In a ball park with a capacity of 33,379, Boston's attendance perennially flirts with the two-million mark and is always near the top of both leagues. Yet the club has won only two pennants in over fifty-five years.

During one six-year period after World War II, the Red Sox were annual favorites nationally to win the American League pennant—and didn't win one. In two successive years they lost on the last day of the season, once in a playoff, the other time by losing two straight games in Yankee Stadium.

They once kept two-thirds of New England and most of the Maritimes up until two in the morning listening to an extra-inning game. Commercial pilots flying that night between Boston and Yarmouth, Nova Scotia, reported lights on in houses all the way up. One flier later announced that the lights all went out at once as soon as the game ended. He knew because he was listening to it himself.

Two sure barroom brawl subjects were always Ted Williams and Tom Yawkey. Take either side and you could find an argument. The pros and cons of these two individuals are as well defined as those of the ball club they represent.

The hysteria of Red Sox fans is an old phenomenon in New England, for Boston was one of baseball's earliest strongholds. And even though the team that later became known as the Braves preceded the Red Sox by a quarter century, Boston was never really a Braves town. The Red Sox were actually named for the National League team that had a twenty-five-year headstart on it, for the original Braves were known as the Boston Red Stockings. This fact alone hardly accounts for the fans' long-term preference for the Red Sox. What does is that the Red Sox were winners from the start. They were baseball's first world champions as we know baseball champions today, for they won history's first World Series, in 1903. And during a golden age that lasted from 1912 to 1918, they also won four pennants.

Going back to the early years of this century, the Braves took the play away from the Red Sox only once. That was 1914, when an amazing Braves team, last in July, came on not only to win the National League pennant but to complete the first World Series sweep by taking all four games from the then mighty Philadelphia Athletics.

But from the standpoint of fan loyalty, even that feat didn't help the Braves over the long haul. They didn't win another pennant for thirty-four years. Although the Red Sox also eventually suffered a long dry spell, they followed the 1914 season by winning three of the next four pennants and world championships, which solidified their hold on Boston's—and its hinterlands'—baseball public.

The crowning humiliation for the Braves came in 1948 when they drew 100,000 fewer fans than the Red Sox in a year they won a pennant and the Red Sox didn't. From then on, it was downhill for the Braves, climaxed by their 1952 move to Milwaukee, leaving the New England area to the Red Sox.

No one asked what was wrong with the Red Sox between 1912 and 1918. And in the years immediately following 1918 no one had to ask. Harry Frazee, a Broadway show producer, bought control of the club and sold off all the stars to the Yankees. One, a remarkable pitcher named Babe Ruth, went to New York in return for a few nondescript players and a huge mortgage on Fenway Park.

If Babe Ruth had been left in Boston, who knows what might have happened? A great pitcher became a great slugger and transformed the face of baseball and the locale of its most consistently powerful team. Instead of being perennial winners, as they might have been with Ruth, the Red Sox became perennial losers—with no one asking why.

The team hit bottom in the twenties and early thirties, finishing last for six straight years, and in all, nine years out of eleven. Since the Braves were either seventh or eighth (both leagues had eight clubs in those days) during the same period, the whole Boston baseball picture was dismal enough to have killed the game forever in that city.

For the two major leagues, those were dark days indeed. The city had nine or ten daily newspapers then, but not one reporter on any of them would have thought of entering the team's quarters before or after a game. Although the teams, who could hardly afford it, paid the freight for writers, none traveled with either team except to enjoy the pleasures of spring training. After that, writers and players seldom met until the next spring training.

The day was to come when more members of the media would storm the Red Sox locker room than there were players inside. When traded to Boston from the St. Louis Browns in 1948, Al Zarilla, an outfielder who enjoyed fleeting moments of success, looked at the mob around him after his first game at home, muttered, "My God, I've never been interviewed by so many people in all my life," and fled to the showers. And in the early fifties, a long-time Boston baseball writer was taken off the Red Sox beat for repeating a private locker room conversation between players during spring training. Twenty years earlier, that writer would have been at the beach or on the golf course or, if he'd overheard the conversation, wouldn't have bothered to repeat it.

Boston writers of the generation that began with the twenties considered themselves part of the team. In 1946, a veteran writer, who was called to Tom Yawkey's suite just before the Red Sox clinched their first pennant in twenty-eight years, confided to me, "After next year Joe Cronin [then the manager] will become general manager and Joe McCarthy [recently resigned manager of the Yankees] will manage the Red Sox."

"Why don't you write it?" I asked.

"And get in wrong with Yawkey?"

It came to pass just as my colleague had predicted. After the 1947 season, Cronin became general manager and McCarthy manager. But the story never did break prematurely, even though every old-time Boston baseball writer had it straight from the horse's mouth more than a year in advance. Why, you might ask, didn't I write it? Maybe I should have. But I got it secondhand from a writer on my own paper, and I wasn't that strong with Yawkey that I could have elicited from him anything but a flat denial.

That incident illustrates something else about the Boston Red Sox: while they had one set of writers in their pocket, there was a new generation, of which I was part, that they couldn't quite trust. That led to trouble, trouble I can easily laugh about now, but it was no laughing matter then.

In the early days of the Yawkey regime, the Red Sox needed no public-relations man. The whole Boston press handled their public relations for them. And, while I can't condone the press for doing that, I can understand why it happened.

Before Yawkey, at least from 1919 to 1933, the last place to find anything of sports interest to write about was Fenway Park. The next to last place was Braves Field. The general effect of the team's constant defeats, combined with poor attendance by the fans, was indifference on the part of the writers. They watched the games—only at home —because they had to. Except for a hard core of gamblers in the right field stands, betting on anything from whether or not the batter would swing at the next pitch to the number of innings in which each team would score runs, the stands at both ball parks were practically empty.

But the fans, although latent, were there. They didn't go to the games, but they wrote and phoned the newspapers like mad. All they needed to really get them going was some hope for the future.

They got it when Yawkey bought the Red Sox. The depression was in its worst stage; nobody but a man of Yawkey's means could afford the luxury of a big-league franchise, especially one as rundown as the Red Sox. However, this young Yale graduate just turned thirty must have been the hottest baseball fan of all time. In the years between 1933 and World War II he spent millions in a futile quest for what was to him the pot of gold at the end of the rainbow—at the least an American League pennant, at the most a world championship.

He bought so much talent and built so rapidly that four of his five teams between 1938 and 1942 finished second, always to the Yankees. And it was in those days, with Joe Cronin managing the club, himself a pickup from the Washington Senators for a record price of a quarter of a million dollars (even to this day no single player has ever cost that much), that the lament, "What's the matter with the Red Sox?" was born.

How could a team lose pennant after pennant with stars like Cronin, Jimmy Foxx, Lefty Grove, Wes Ferrell, Eric McNair, Rube Walberg, Heinie Manush, Roger Cramer, Ben Chapman, Bing Miller, Joe Vosmik, and a host of lesser lights in the lineup? Who was to blame— Cronin, the boy wonder, who in his twenties had led the Senators to a pennant and was for years the best shortstop in the business? Eddie Collins, the general manager, hand-picked by Yawkey, builder of this instant powerhouse, who on a single scouting trip to San Diego discovered both Ted Williams and Bobby Doerr? Yawkey himself, the most open-handed owner that baseball had ever known? Were the Yankees that good? Was McCarthy that much better than Cronin as a manager? Was New York's G. M., Ed Barrow, superior to Collins?

These were some of the questions that gave rise to the most baffling question of all—What's the matter with the Red Sox? Boston fans asked it in the late thirties, the forties, the fifties, and the sixties. What happened before World War II was really only the beginning; the question didn't settle in as a chronic complaint until after the war.

Now, in the seventies, the fans are still asking the same question. Yet twice recently, in 1967 and 1972, the Red Sox reversed the trend. In neither year were they expected to go anywhere. The 1966 team had finished ninth, but the 1967 team, the team of the Impossible Dream, captured the hearts of Red Sox fans and baseball followers all over the country. Carl Yastrzemski blossomed into the superstar he had much earlier promised to become. Manager Dick Williams, young, brash, virtually unknown, led the team to glory. They won the pennant—the first time that a big-league team had ever jumped from ninth place to first in one year.

The 1972 team, third of six clubs in the American League East division, and eighteen games from the top at the end of the 1971 season, had little hope of improving their position. But after such a bad start that by midseason there seemed even less hope, they suddenly woke up and came within twenty-four hours of winning the division title. On the next to last day of the season, the club lost to Detroit by half a game.

But before that, the old cry, "What's the matter with the Red Sox?" had drowned out all the other baseball noises around Boston, while the club itself, listless and lackadaisical until early August, had just about drowned out baseball.

The man who woke it up was a sensational rookie catcher, Carlton (Pudge) Fisk. In an interview with Gene McCormick of the Springfield (Mass.) *Union* on August 7, 1972, Fisk innocently caused an uproar by charging, among other things, that the Red Sox weren't getting proper leadership from their veterans, specifically Carl Yastrzemski and Reggie Smith. After a painful day in the Red Sox locker room when the story broke in the Boston papers, Fisk, a soft-spoken country boy from Charlestown, N.H., made his peace with his older teammates, and the ball club thereupon caught fire.

Before Labor Day, the Red Sox were in the midst of a mad battle for the division lead, with Baltimore and New York as well as Detroit. The battle lasted the whole month of September, during most of which the Red Sox were in first place. Their fans, hardly able to believe that this 1972 team could be a reincarnation of the 1967 club, waited until the last week of the season before really storming the gates of Fenway Park.

By then, 1972 looked so much like 1967 that all of the northeast was once again under the spell of a baseball team that had gone from awful to sensational in less than two months. When the Red Sox announced the date that play-off tickets would go on sale, a Boston restaurant served the young fan who was first in line a full-course meal, complete with table and tablecloth, the evening before. That was followed by a 1:00 A.M. steak dinner, once again presented right on the Jersey Street sidewalk in front of the

Fenway Park ticket offices. The city and all its satellite towns suddenly went crazy.

Deprived of their two best pitchers (Sonny Siebert, who'd gone sour, and Ray Culp, with a flagging arm), the Red Sox had come up with a whole new rotation of four hurlers. Luis Tiant, a Cuban veteran of many seasons in many places, rediscovered magic in his ancient right arm and became the ace of the staff, after winning one and losing seven the year before. The other three were Marty Pattin, who had come to Boston the previous autumn in a trade, and a couple of rookies, Lynn McGlothen and John Curtis.

The rest of the team was a mixture of young and old hands, who blended like vodka and tonic. The field leadership was provided by Fisk himself. In the dugout, Manager Eddie Kasko, colorless but efficient, got the most out of everyone by juggling, shifting and, with the help of Lee Stange, his pitching coach, squeezing the last drop of use out of his throwers.

The fact that the Impossible Dream had its rude awakening so late in the season only whetted the appetites of the ever-loyal Red Sox fans. The dust of the deciding 1972 game had hardly settled in Detroit when they began talking about next year.

It is not the first time, nor will it be the last. "Next year" has been the answer to the eternal question, "What's the matter with the Red Sox?" for the forty years that Tom Yawkey has owned the club.

As we shall see, even though nothing was the matter with the Red Sox in 1946, the seed of future problems was sown then. Don't ask me why. It just happened that way.

But that is why I now pose the question from that point in time. Maybe the events of 1946 and the years that followed will provide the answers.

—Al Hirshberg

Pocasset, Massachusetts
September 1972

Contents

WHAT'S THE MATTER WITH THE RED SOX?

CHAPTER 1

Dynasty Hopes

The year 1946 was the happiest that baseball ever knew. At last World War II was over, which had absorbed the largest number of able-bodied men over the widest age range in American history. Virtually every man between eighteen and forty-five who could pass a physical examination went into the service or was engaged in essential industry. Before the war ended in August of 1945, practically all ballplayers of major-league caliber were in factories or wearing unfamiliar uniforms.

Except for the St. Louis Cardinals, who had several outstanding ballplayers with just enough physical ailments to keep them out of the service, no team had many bona fide big leaguers. Most of the men who played between 1943 and 1945 were a ragtag and bobtail collection. This period found the St. Louis Browns with a one-armed outfielder, and other clubs loaded with cripples, semi-cripples, pot-bellied time-clock punchers, service rejects, elder baseball statesmen reluctantly making emergency comebacks on the field, and Class C ballplayers play-acting as big leaguers.

The game couldn't have survived without them. It did survive because President Franklin D. Roosevelt wanted it to, as he indicated when he gave the game the green light in 1942. But it was a green light for professional baseball, not necessarily for its able-bodied players. The best of these were absorbed into the service along with their able-bodied contemporaries in other walks of life.

Every club in the majors stood ready to welcome ballplayers who were released from the service because of physical ailments. One of the most impressive of these was a tall, soft-spoken Mississippi boy named Dave (Boo) Ferriss, whom the Red Sox picked up after the discomforts of chronic asthma released him from the army. Ferriss, whose remarkable abilities in baseball were known only to God and a couple of Red Sox scouts before he got out of the service, quickly became a Boston favorite. The young man was essentially a right-handed pitcher. But in 1945 while he was in the process of winning twenty-one games for the seventh-place Red Sox (in an eight-club league), wild stories filtered down about his Bunyanesque exploits in prewar baseball leagues of various description.

Ferriss could, as he proved that year, hit a baseball fantastic distances—when he got hold of one. He could, according to rumor, throw as well with his left arm as his right. Some of the stories told of him were too good to be true. When he wasn't pitching right-handed he could play first base left-handed. It was said that he had often moved to first base after being knocked out of the box right-handed, and stayed in the game left-handed because of his potent bat. He had—and this, too, was unconfirmed rumor —even pitched part of a game with his right arm and the rest with his left.

Rumor or no rumor, there was no question of his ability to pitch right-handed. Ferriss was one of the few wartime pitchers who seemed sure of making it big when peace brought all the legitimate big leaguers back into baseball's fold. After the war, the Red Sox brass included him in the plans for 1946, which would be the first full-season peacetime year for baseball since 1941.

Baseball normalcy began in the spring of 1946 when all sixteen major-league clubs then in operation returned to their spring training bases in Florida or the west. During the war they had done their training in local baseball cages or nearby resorts where snow was least likely.

In those days the Red Sox were known as Yawkey's Millionaires, for if Tom Yawkey had any faults, reluctance to spend a buck was not one of them. Undoubtedly the most generous owner in baseball, he gave maximum reward for minimum performance. He was, in fact, too open-handed with the men he paid for playing baseball. While other magnates cut financial corners wherever they could, doling out every salary dollar as if it were their last, Yawkey threw money at his hired hands. It was rumored—and I believe it —that he never cut a salary. When a player had a bad year, he either didn't get a raise or was traded or sent to the minors.

The result of Yawkey's generosity was a universal desire on the part of ballplayers everywhere to play for this prince of good fellows and most rabid of fans. Yawkey was a frank, unblushing hero-worshipper. In the early days of his stewardship at Fenway Park, nothing gave him more pleasure than to put on a Red Sox uniform and work out with the Jimmy Foxxes and Joe Cronins and Lefty Groves who toiled for him. He virtually lived with them during the season and invited them to his South Carolina island to hunt in winter.

But by 1946, although his enthusiasm for baseball was as hot as ever, it was noticed that he had stopped playing big brother to his ballplayers. Not that he was any less generous with them. But a new generation had arrived, a generation hardened by war experiences (whether or not they had seen combat), and, at first, more practical than their predecessors in their approach to baseball.

But the change in attitude was more on Yawkey's part than theirs. The Foxxes and the Groves were out of baseball, and Cronin functioned purely as a bench manager, not a playing manager. The close ties of friendship between owner and players were disappearing, because the owner was now well out of their age orbit. By the end of World War II Yawkey was forty-three and his ballplayers were in their twenties.

He still enjoyed playing ball, but no longer spent time on the field or in the locker room with members of the team. Instead, when in Boston, which was most of the time between May and October, he played mornings with whoever happened to be around: from clubhouse boys, groundskeepers, and ushers, to occasional passersby who simply dropped by to see what was going on.

But there was a difference. In the old days Yawkey hung around the locker room for hours being one of the boys. Now, when he finished working out, he showered, dressed, and disappeared, usually into the front office. While keeping closely informed of what was going on, Yawkey was losing the personal touch with his ballplayers that had characterized the earlier years of his ownership.

Something else was happening, something so subtle that it did not become apparent for several years. The effervescent young owner who fraternized so freely with everyone around the ball park was beginning a new life phase, crawling into a shell of privacy which for some years made him very nearly a recluse. He did not appear in Sarasota, Florida, for spring training in 1946 and thereafter did so very rarely. Even at owners' meetings he was usually represented by his general manager of the moment.

The ballplayers who reported to Manager Joe Cronin for spring training in 1946 were as good, if not better than the expensive stars of prewar years. The top man, as he had been since his rookie year of 1939, was the last of the .400 hitters, the great, tempestuous, and quixotic Ted Williams. Except for Cronin himself, Williams was one of the very few ballplayers still privileged to call Yawkey "Tom." (To most, he had become "T.A." or "Mr. Yawkey," as he is now to everyone except his old associates.)

Williams's privileges went well beyond calling his employer by his first name. As one of baseball's superstars, he was given preferential treatment, to which, of course, he was entitled. One of these was the option of handling newspapermen in any way he saw fit. And Ted Williams traditionally saw fit to treat the Boston press—with two notable exceptions—as human beings in the spring and as dogs from Labor Day on.

The battle between Williams and the Boston press has

been hashed over many times by everyone, including Williams himself. Yet the Boston press, despite its freedom to write of him as its members liked, never properly defended itself. I was part of that press for some years—through the 1952 season to be precise—after which I became a full-time freelance writer.

It was not my privilege to go south with Boston's clubs before World War II, but I came into frequent contact with players on both teams during the season, when I functioned as an occasional columnist for the very late lamented Boston *Post*. In common with many of my colleagues I found Ted Williams the most aggravating and most interesting personality in baseball.

During his rookie year of 1939, he was a happy kid playing a boys' game with grown men. At twenty, he bubbled with enthusiasm, an engaging young six-foot-three giant who was so thin he seemed all arms and legs. Except for his swing, a marvel of smooth power, he was as physically awkward as any other boy of his age and build. He didn't really run; he galloped, bouncing up and down like a little girl skipping rope, yet covering huge chunks of ground with each great stride.

This gait was to become part of his undoing, for, even when running hardest he never seemed to be working at it. I don't believe he was slower or tried any less intensely than most other ballplayers, but he *looked* slower because he was so awkward. Worse, he looked as if he wasn't trying, which was why, once his feud with the press began, he was so often accused of loafing.

Yet Williams's first brush in Boston was not with the press but with the fans. He played right field his rookie year, and right field at Fenway Park was, as it still is, the area closest to the stands. At the very start of Williams's career, he was the special darling of Boston's right field fans. They cheered everything he did, especially his home runs. In fact, the man who later became famous for his refusal to tip his cap, showed his appreciation with grins, waves, and frequent sweeps of appreciation with his hat in his hand.

As a left-handed batter, Williams's power alley was right field, so those homers all had to be tremendous wallops at Fenway Park. In those days, the distance from the plate to the right field bleachers was over 400 feet along the foul line. Since Williams hit thirty-one homers as a rookie, and more than half were at home, none were cheap shots. But after the 1939 season, home and visiting bullpens were built in front of the right field bleachers, and the field was turned far enough to the right to put that sector of the grandstand into fair territory, giving a left-handed pull hitter a better shot at a home run to right. The Red Sox announced that this change was for Williams's benefit, so that area was known for years as "Williamstown."

Earlier though, in fact about three months after the 1939 season began, came the first step in the breakdown of the love affair between Williams and the Boston fans. It all started when Williams, playing right field, let a ground ball go through his legs. When he turned to chase it, his awkward gallop made it appear that he wasn't running as fast as he could. When he finally reached the ball at the right field bleacher fence, he was greeted with a chorus of boos. This swelled into a tremendous Bronx cheer when, after throwing the ball in, Williams turned to yell a few choice obscenities. When he came into the dugout at the end of the inning, he said, "Those sonsofbitches! I'll never tip my cap to them again." And he never did.

Within a week, the two most vitriolic sports columnists in town, Dave Egan of the *Record* and Austen (Duke) Lake of the *American,* had castigated Williams not once, but several times. That completed Williams's disenchantment with Boston, its fans, and its press. I don't believe he ever spoke a civil word to either columnist again. They, in turn, blasted him regularly while rarely finding anything good to say about his play. They even criticized his superb hitting on the grounds that it usually came at times when it helped the ball club least and Williams most.

Williams's transition from hating Egan and Lake to apparently hating the entire Boston press was easy, as was the press's retaliation. But, while almost all Boston writers felt the sting of Williams's scorn at one time or another (except the old-timers who never criticized him in print and stayed away from him to avoid signs of his venom), none but Egan and Lake were permanent residents of his doghouse. Both have long since gone to glory, where, no doubt, they are still proclaiming Williams's shortcomings to ectoplasmic colleagues. I am sure that when Williams's time comes the lifelong feud will become eternal.

While I often found Williams difficult, wrote my share of critical pieces about him, and had frequent occasion to vent what little spleen I had on him, I must admit he was unapproachable only some of the time. I found the easiest way to handle him was to ask a question about hitting. That and fishing were always his favorite subjects, but my curiosity about fish begins and ends at the dinner table. On the other hand, I never tired of listening to Williams talk hitting, for I have no doubt that this man knows more about it than anyone alive or dead, up to and including such late immortals as Ty Cobb, Babe Ruth, and Rogers Hornsby.

I am not even sure Williams hated the Boston press as much as he was supposed to, except for Egan and Lake. He was contemptuous of several members of the press, including, I think, the older men who were openly afraid of him. He disliked criticism in general but respected critics who were fair and logical, which Egan and Lake were not. He enjoyed making the press squirm, and no one could do it with a sharper needle. I still have a vivid memory of the day the Red Sox ballplayers voted to ban the press for an hour after games. When the time was nearly up, Williams, clad only in a towel, stood just inside the locker room door, tolling the seconds of the hour's last minute. Finally, he said, "OK. Now all you bastards can come in." Except for the clubhouse boys, he was the only person in the place.

But in the spring of the year, particularly the year 1946, all was well between the Boston press and Williams as well as his happily cavorting teammates. This was a good ball club at full strength, but followers of the Red Sox were slow to accept that fact at face value; too many good Red Sox ball clubs at full strength had fallen on their faces in the years just before the outbreak of the war.

In reality, this *was* a good team—perhaps a great one. The lineup was nearly set before the club broke camp to barnstorm north by train, as big-league teams did in those days. At first base was the powerful but aging Rudy York, obtained during the winter in a trade with the Tigers. At second was Bobby Doerr, once one of the youngest boys ever to play big-league ball. (He was sixteen when the Red Sox first brought him up.) At short was Johnny Pesky, who in his rookie year, 1942, had collected over 200 hits. Williams was in left. Dominic DiMaggio, youngest member of the clan immortalized by his brother Joe, would have been recognized as great in his own right if he hadn't been overshadowed by a superstar within his immediate family. A fine hitter, he was, in the opinion of many observers, the best center fielder in baseball, better even than Joe. Third base and right field were open, and the catching, handled by Hal Wagner backed up by Roy Partee, was a bit better than average.

The great potential strength of this club was in the pitching staff. Almost all earlier Yawkey teams had been loaded with power and short on pitching. But the 1946 hurlers had more going for them than any Red Sox club in thirty years. They were not recognized as great during spring training, largely because no one could predict with any accuracy the possible effects of two or three years out of baseball.

Even Ferriss was a question mark. While looking the part of a major leaguer in 1945, the fact remained that he hadn't pitched against major-league opposition. Tex Hughson, who had given every indication of being a future ace, looked very good indeed in spring training. So did Jim Bagby, Jr., veteran of an earlier Red Sox era, but Bagby, never a ball of fire, rarely looked bad in spring. Joe Dobson, brought to Boston in a trade with Cleveland, was an unknown quantity. So was Mickey Harris, a fun-loving southpaw, complete with pixie grin and a New York ac-

cent, from Queens Village, Long Island. A lanky, smiling
war hero named Earl Johnson gave promise of a return to
the good form he had occasionally shown before his service days. And Charlie Wagner, a big winner one year before the war, was back on the baseball firing line after
three years in the navy.

On the day before the 1946 season began, the Red Sox
were universally chosen for third place by those who called
themselves experts. The popular favorites, now that everyone was back in the fold, were the New York Yankees, still
managed by Joe McCarthy, who had already taken them
to eight pennants—seven in the eight years from 1936
through 1943. The consensus was that the Tigers, who had
won the pennant and World Series in 1945, would finish
second.

Only one baseball man of high credentials picked the
Red Sox to win the pennant. Manager Lou Boudreau of
the Indians called them the best balanced team in the
American League and, to his way of thinking, definitely
the club to beat.

As always, the Boston press picked the Red Sox for first
place, but this had been an occupational disease of the
Boston press for years. Joe Cronin did the same, which was
understandable. While football coaches fed on the seeds of
pessimism, baseball managers were born optimists and
Cronin was more optimistic than most.

The Red Sox opened in Washington, a day ahead of the
rest of the American League, with President Harry S Truman throwing out the first ball. At third base was a past
and future nonentity named Ernie Andres, who was lucky
to last with the club through Mother's Day. In right field

was a veteran of several teams named George "Cat" Metkovich, a good journeyman ballplayer who had a few years to go before winning immortality as a temporary first baseman with Cleveland. One day, when the visiting White Sox filled the bases with two out in a close game, somebody hit a ground ball which Metkovich stopped but couldn't find. Frantically he looked around his feet for it, as White Sox runners galloped madly around the bases. When Metkovich caught the first base umpire's eye, he yelled, "Well, don't just stand there. Get a glove and help me find it!"

Other lesser names cropped up in this first postwar season. Clem Driesewerd, a relief pitcher of some experience who saved a game here and there. Bill Zuber, born with a German accent into the strictly fundamentalist Amana Society in Iowa and barred from returning because he had deserted "to the outside." Zuber, a relief pitcher whom the Red Sox picked up from the Yankees, had an effective sinker which he described as his "zinker ball." Mace Brown, a veteran pitcher in the final throes of a long, rather undistinguished career. Mike Ryba, a gold-toothed lobby-sitting champion who once played every position in a minor-league game and who, like Brown, was finishing a long major-league career of mediocrity. A former coal miner, Ryba never stopped marveling at the joys of big-league baseball, which he appreciated more than most. Leon Culberson, an outfielder and third baseman cursed with a name so similar to the nationally famous bridge expert, Ely Culbertson, that he was forever begging writers please to leave out the "t." Mike Higgins, bought from the Tigers in his last big-league year to plug the hole at third base, which he did very well. Eddie Pellagrini, a

local boy who, although a good infielder, could not hit
big-league pitching, even though he slammed a home run
his first time at bat in the majors. Don Gutteridge and Rip
Russell, two good infield refugees from the National
League, who competently plugged holes wherever they
happened to crop up. And Tom McBride, an outfielder
whom Cronin platooned with Metkovich.

Charlie Wagner, permanently weakened by dysentery
picked up in the South Pacific, could no longer pitch, but
the Red Sox kept him because he was a cheerful character
whose sense of humor and sharp dress gave him more class
than most. Besides, he was Ted Williams's favorite (and
last) roommate.

These were the men who, in one way or another, shared
in the glory of the 1946 season. It all began with a typical
Red Sox opening day in Washington; even the president
got a hint of what was to come that year. In Washington's
ancient Griffith Stadium, Tex Hughson won a 6–3 victory
in which the Red Sox collected eleven hits, including a
mammoth home run by Ted Williams, which traveled
nearly 500 feet into dead center field.

The next day, although Ferriss was knocked out of the
box after four innings, the Red Sox won a 13–6 game behind the relief pitching of Earl Johnson. Williams had two
doubles and a single in three official at bats and Dom Di-
Maggio had two for four, drove in four runs, and hit an
inside-the-park home run. Mickey Harris beat the Senators,
3–1, to sweep the series on the third day. In that game
Williams had another homer, and Pesky got three hits in
five times up.

Even at that early stage, the pattern was beginning to

emerge—victories for Hughson and Harris, a relief victory for Johnson, Williams hitting home runs, DiMaggio and Pesky collecting their share of hits. When the Red Sox opened at home, they were undefeated in three games.

Hughson made it four straight by shutting out the Philadelphia Athletics. The next day, in the first game of a doubleheader at Fenway Park, Dobson made it five in a row in relief of Ferriss. That broke the pattern, for it marked one of the few times Ferriss was knocked out twice in a row and one of the rare relief appearances for Dobson. The Athletics, however, finally stopped the Red Sox streak by beating them in the second game, cut to five innings by rain.

Pellagrini hit his career-opening home run the next day, when he went in to replace Pesky, who had been knocked out of action for a day or two when hit by a pitch thrown by Sid Hudson of the Senators. Harris won that one, 5–4. So after seven games, the Red Sox had won six, lost one, and were leading the league. Two of the big four pitchers (Ferriss had nothing to show after two starts, and Dobson's only victory was in relief) were beginning to stand out. Hughson and Harris each had two victories without a defeat.

On April 25, just behind the Tigers and the Yankees, the Red Sox began an amazing streak that actually wrapped up the pennant before the middle of May. It started when Dobson beat the Yankees, 12–5, and Ferriss followed with his first victory, a 7–0 shutout over the A's in Philadelphia. Hughson and Harris then pitched the team back into first place with a doubleheader victory in Philly. That was on April 28. From then on, Boston was never out of the lead.

They won fifteen straight games, ripping through Detroit, Cleveland, St. Louis, and Chicago, finally winning the fifteenth in a row over the Yankees in New York. That was on May 10, leaving the Red Sox with twenty-one victories against only three defeats. The figures both for the pitchers and for hitters were awesome.

The big four, Harris, Dobson, Ferriss, and Hughson, had won fifteen games and lost one (an April defeat of Hughson by the Yankees). Williams was batting .409 with five homers, Pesky .406, DiMaggio .387, Hal Wagner .340, Culberson .326, York .318, and Metkovich .302.

When the Yankees finally stopped them on May 11, Dave Egan blamed the loss on Williams, who had looked at one of his rare third strikes with a couple of men on base and played a fly ball to left into a triple when he misjudged it. At this criticism Williams justifiably blew his stack, for he knew as well as anyone that the Red Sox wouldn't have been where they were without him.

Harris beat the Yankees the next day for his sixth straight victory, putting his team five and a half games in front of the pack, and it began to be pretty obvious that nobody in the American League was going to take them that year.

They murdered the Senators in a doubleheader just before the All-Star break, with Hughson winning the opener, 11–1, and Driesewerd in relief taking the second game, 9–4. Almost everybody had good days at the plate, and the natural result was that the Red Sox piled up thirty hits in the two games. In the first game, Williams went four for six, including his twenty-third homer, and walked five times in the two games combined. The rest of the club did its share—two doubles and a single for Metkovich, a double and three singles for Pesky, two doubles and three singles for DiMaggio, a triple in one game and a homer in the other for Hal Wagner, five hits in ten times up for York.

The Red Sox figures at the All-Star break, individually and collectively, were as startling as after their fifteen-game streak in April and May. They had won fifty-four out of seventy-seven games and were a comfortable seven and a half in front of the second-place Yankees. Dom DiMaggio was second among the American League batters at .349, and Williams third, two points behind. But Williams, besides his twenty-three home runs, had seventy-two runs batted in, a figure matched by Bobby Doerr, who was now going strong after a slow start. Doerr had eleven homers, York ten. Although batting .269, York had sixty-one RBIs and was third in that department behind the tied league leaders, Williams and Doerr.

The pitching was just as impressive: Ferriss twelve and four, Harris eleven and four, Dobson eight and three, Hughson nine and five. While Driesewerd had four victories without a loss in relief, and Johnson was four and two.

The All-Star game was in Boston that year, and Williams put on a dazzling one-man show for the home folks. He paced the American League to a 12–0 trouncing of the National, collecting two homers and two singles, his four hits topping the whole National League team combined, which collected only three. Williams's second homer was off the so-called eephus, or blooper ball, thrown by Rip Sewell of the Pirates, a pitch that required the hitter to supply all the power. Sewell would toss the ball high in the air and make it float down squarely over the plate. When

Williams put it into the visiting bullpen in right field, it was the only time anyone ever drove it out of the park.

By the end of July the Red Sox were twelve games ahead of the Yankees and thirteen ahead of the Tigers. A month later they still led the field by thirteen and a half; Ferriss had twenty-three victories, Hughson eighteen, Harris fifteen, and Dobson eleven. Among the regulars were five .300 hitters and three with more than 100 RBIs, while Williams had thirty-four homers, Doerr eighteen, and York fifteen.

When the Red Sox won both ends of a doubleheader from the Yankees in New York on September 2 (Ferriss's twenty-fourth and Harris's sixteenth), they moved fifteen and a half games in front with twenty left to play. Everything seemed hunky-dory, but there were a few little clouds. Three days before, Williams, for reasons best known to himself, had blown his stack in a game against the Athletics. Once he refused to run out an infield roller, and later he threw first his glove, then the ball, accompanying both gestures with a stream of invective directed at nobody in particular.

Perhaps it was Dave Egan and Duke Lake, both of whom continued to bait him unmercifully. It could even have been the late Hy Hurwitz of the Boston *Globe*, who packed more guts into his five-foot-one frame than most men a foot taller. Hurwitz, a former marine combat correspondent, was one of the few prewar Boston baseball writers who stood up to Williams and anyone else who happened to annoy him. By then he and Williams had a private feud of their own going. The *Globe* had hired Williams to give his own day-by-day impressions of this apparent pennant-winning season and had assigned Hurwitz to ghostwrite them. The matchup wasn't a week old before the two were at each other's throats. Around the seventh inning of every game, press box colleagues began hearing some choice Marine Corps language, with Hurwitz muttering such bits as, "In two more innings I'm going to have to go down to listen to that big sonofabitch." At the same time, ballplayers on the bench would be hearing Williams bark, "In two more innings I'm going to have to talk to that nogood little bastard." Hardly a marriage made in heaven.

During the same period, the usually mild Cronin was carrying on a feud of his own with Huck Finnegan, the Boston *American* baseball writer who traveled with the Red Sox. Finnegan, a colleague of Lake's, had for years been telling all who would listen that Cronin was a lousy manager. As they traveled the American League circuit by train in 1946, the two had plenty of time to bend each other's ear. Whenever they met, they exchanged insults, Cronin crowing and Finnegan fuming. Once, sitting at adjacent tables in the dining car, Finnegan yelled so much invective across the aisle that Cronin brandished a steak knife at him.

Here was a team running away with a pennant in the first peacetime season in four years, yet bickering between press and ball club had become standard operating procedure. Everyone in the Red Sox orbit was already taking the pennant for granted, and at the rate they were going the Red Sox could probably clinch it in the first ten days of September.

Most of the players stayed out of the firing line. The

greatest fussing and feuding was between Williams and the media, with Cronin and Finnegan getting their own two cents worth in. The atmosphere of animosity may have directly concerned only a few of the Red Sox people, but everyone on the ball club as well as the entire press corps, which had grown to about thirty New Englanders, plus fifteen or twenty out-of-towners assigned to cover their clinching of the pennant, expected an explosion any minute.

The abrasive situation was intensified by an unexpected series of frustrations, during which the Red Sox, miles ahead of the field, went into a temporary nose dive that prevented them from administering the *coup de grace.* Consequently, everybody in the traveling Red Sox party was a bundle of nerves.

On September 8, Ferriss was beaten in Philadelphia while both the Yankees and the Tigers were dropping doubleheaders; so the "magic number" for the Red Sox was one. In other words, to clinch the pennant, they needed just one more victory combined with one Tiger defeat. They were seventeen games ahead of Detroit, with the Yankees out of the running. But the defeat in Philadelphia was the third in a row for the Red Sox, who picked this point in the pennant race to go into a slump.

September 9 was an off day. On the tenth, about five hours before the Red Sox opened a two-day series in Detroit, World Series tickets went on sale at Fenway Park. Since the team could clinch with a victory either day, Tom Yawkey went to Detroit, while Tom Dowd, the traveling secretary, ordered champagne for a victory party.

Mickey Harris started the September 10 game, but that

was just about all he did. While he was blowing sky high, the Red Sox were busy losing one opportunity after another. They filled the bases with one out in the first inning, but failed to score. They also failed after filling the bases with nobody out in the eighth. But by then Harris was long gone, and so were the Red Sox. The Tigers tore them apart, 9–1. The only Red Sox run of the afternoon was Ted Williams's thirty-sixth homer of the season.

The champagne remained stashed in its cases, and the Red Sox, riding a four-game losing streak, went into the Detroit game of September 11 sixteen games in front. Boo Ferriss pitched that afternoon, but he should have stayed home. For instead of clinching the pennant, Ferriss lost a 7–3 decision. Now, the Red Sox were only fifteen games in front, with the elusive pennant still dangling right in front of their noses.

"You'll blow it," Finnegan told Cronin.

"The hell with you," Cronin retorted.

Nobody, not even Finnegan, thought the Red Sox would blow it, but it looked as if their fight to clinch would go on indefinitely. They left Detroit with their magic number still one and moved on to Cleveland, needing help. Even if they beat the Indians, the Yankees, in Detroit, would have to beat the Tigers.

It was a sullen, unhappy collection of ballplayers who checked into Cleveland's Statler-Hilton Hotel on the night of the eleventh. What happened to the champagne in Detroit was never announced. It probably stayed there.

On the twelfth, the Red Sox threw Jim Bagby, Jr. against Bob Feller in Cleveland's ancient League Park, where the Indians then played their weekday games. It was no contest. Feller toyed with the Red Sox, beating them, 4–1, for their sixth straight loss. In the meantime the Tigers beat the Yankees in Detroit, leaving them fourteen games behind.

By this time, most of the newspapermen were snickering, as the players stayed conspicuously out of sight. Since television was in its infancy, ballplayers were still among the world's most devoted lobby-sitters, but few did any lobby-sitting that night in Cleveland. They kept in their rooms, went to the movies, or popped into nearby bars to try to drown their sorrows, which, despite their still huge lead, were becoming deeper and deeper.

Now it was September 13, and the Red Sox went to League Park again in hopes that this might be the day. The game began at one o'clock Eastern Daylight Time, which was noon, Eastern Standard Time, in Detroit. Tex Hughson was on the mound for the beleaguered Red Sox. Opposing him was Red Embree, a good journeyman pitcher capable of heights that approached greatness.

Embree quickly disposed of the first two Boston hitters in the first inning, bringing Williams up with two out and the bases empty. Manager Lou Boudreau of the Indians, inventor of what was then known as the "Williams shift," moved his players around accordingly. Everyone swung to the right, leaving the left side of the diamond empty, except for Pat Seerey, the left fielder, who came in so close that he was practically playing a deep shortstop.

Cleveland's League Park had a very deep left field— nearly 400 feet—and a fairly short fence in right field. Like most managers when their clubs faced the Red Sox, Boudreau guarded Williams's power alley heavily and virtually gave him the left side of the diamond. Despite his homer in Detroit, the slugger was in a slump himself. Ordinarily, he would have tried to pull the ball, especially in a park where, if he hit one solidly, it would go so far that nobody on the packed right side could field it.

But Seerey was all alone on the left side, and the fat Cleveland outfielder was a notoriously slow runner. For the first time since Boudreau had started the shift in midseason, Williams deliberately squared away at the plate and hit an Embree pitch high over Seerey's head. The ball landed about where Seerey might have caught it playing a normal left field, and as the heavy-footed Cleveland outfielder started after it, it rolled all the way to the fence.

This precipitated a frantic, side-splitting race which looked like a sprint between a hippopotamus and a giraffe. Williams bounded around the bases in his typical gallop, while Seerey huffed and puffed in the opposite direction after the ball, now resting comfortably against the left field fence. He reached it before Williams reached third, and Joe Cronin, who was coaching there, waved Williams on. Now puffing heavily himself, the long, lean Red Sox slugger pounded toward the plate as Boudreau, taking the throw from the exhausted Seerey, turned and made a great line peg to his catcher, Jim Hegan. Williams, who probably didn't slide five times a year, hit the dirt, beat the throw by a whisker, and completed the only inside-the-park homer of his entire big league career.

The Red Sox thereupon resumed their week-old slump. Except for a single by Johnny Pesky, they didn't get another hit off Red Embree. However, they didn't need one. Hughson, pitching as well as his opponent, held the Indians to three scattered hits, and Williams's wondrous home run stood up for a 1–0 victory.

This took them almost, but not quite, to the pennant. They still needed a Detroit defeat to clinch. But, because of the time differential between Cleveland and Detroit, and the fact that Detroit's game began at 2:00 P.M. Detroit time, they had to wait several hours before they would know. Their game in Cleveland ended two minutes before the game between the Yankees and the Tigers was to begin in Detroit. The Red Sox sweated it out while showering and dressing, sweated it more while riding from the Cleveland ball park to the hotel, and were still sweating it when they arrived at the Statler-Hilton.

The lobby was jammed with insurance agents and executives from all over the country, in town for a national convention. A few of the ballplayers lost themselves in the crowd, a few more went to nearby bars to drink and listen to the Detroit game on the radio, and the rest disappeared into their rooms. When, at last, the news came that the Yankees had won and the Red Sox were finally, painfully in, the whole team was scattered.

Joe Cronin got into an elevator at one floor of the hotel, and Huck Finnegan entered the same elevator at another.

"Well," Cronin growled, "what do you say now, you bleeping bastard?"

"You'll never win another," Finnegan growled back.

The elevator door opened at the lobby just in time for a waiting contingent of insurance people to hear the final words of this exchange. The manager of the new American League champions and future American League president, fists clenched and face red with rage, grunted, "Bleep you,

Finnegan." And Finnegan, in a rare burst of originality, retorted, "Bleep you, Cronin."

This was the first public announcement by both the Red Sox and its press following the clinching of the pennant. As the two angry men stomped out of the elevator, the flower of the American insurance profession stepped aside in shocked silence to make room for them.

From then on, mutual contempt between players and writers was the motif, and profanity its usual means of expression. No one ever found out whose idea it was, but unlike most pennant-winning parties on the road, which are shared by players and traveling writers, the Red Sox held one for the athletes and a separate one for the press. This served only to fan the flames of journalistic resentment to a fever pitch. From a public relations standpoint, the Red Sox would have been much better off to simply bar the press altogether.

I was in the press party along with the rest of the pariahs. We all felt like scullery maids, banished to the kitchen while the lords and masters enjoyed themselves in the main dining room. The food and liquor were good, but our mood was nasty indeed.

It all came to a head quickly, but everyone was too angry and too smashed to savor its full aroma. Tom Yawkey, possibly trying to make up for what he knew had been a ridiculous blunder, came to fraternize and remained to argue. He and Duke Lake got into a shouting match which rivaled the exchange between Cronin and Finnegan and nearly erupted into a fist fight.

Somewhere along the line it was disclosed that Ted Williams was not at the players' party. While everyone speculated—many of us in print—about the big star of the new champions ducking his own victory party, a story circulated that he was visiting a dying wartime buddy. This may have been true, but the combined insult to the writers by both Williams and the Red Sox front office was the first real shot of a long and bitter war.

If I seem to be putting too much emphasis on the press, there's a reason for my madness. From 1946 on, there *was* too much emphasis on the press. The Red Sox front office simply couldn't make up its mind where it stood: whether to ignore the writers or to shower them with food, liquor, and gifts—everything, in fact, but respect.

Is that what was wrong with the Red Sox? Partly. Wholly? Definitely not. There were too many other factors. But one thing is certain. The press could have—and perhaps would have—helped the ball club instead of beating its brains out at every opportunity, if the front office had been reasonable and consistent in its treatment of the press corps. The Red Sox just didn't know how to make the press work for them, and the result was a multitude of unnecessary problems. The ball club's failure to solve these problems was to cost Tom Yawkey millions and the team at least two pennants.

CHAPTER 2

The Wall

Although I have been patiently briefed time and again by various Red Sox officials, including managers, general managers, experienced observers, and even ballplayers, I have never understood just why for so many years the Red Sox felt they must have a big, powerful, right-handed hitting first baseman. Perhaps I am stupid. Perhaps the Red Sox are. Or perhaps we're all smart and the ball park is stupid. For the emphasis that has always been placed on this big right-handed slugger for a first baseman is inspired by the peculiar layout of Fenway Park.

The Boston ball park, a cozy little yard holding less than 34,000 people (although they once jammed over 41,000 into it by roping off the outfield) is one of the few remaining major-league emporiums with character. While most baseball towns now have huge stadiums that all look very much alike, with symmetrical dimensions, Fenway Park is attractively lopsided.

Although it is only 302 feet down the right field foul line, the line breaks so sharply at that point that only a well-placed billiard shot will go into the stands for a home run. The average distance from the plate to right field—in the area of the bullpens built for Ted Williams—is 382 feet. But the distance from the plate to left field is only 315 feet, and the fence there breaks out so slowly that any right-handed pull hitter has a good shot at it almost to center field. Known as the Wall, this fence is the terror of south-paw pitchers, a thing of beauty and a constant joy for long-hitting right-handed batters.

The Wall is the cause of as much grief as pleasure, and may be one of the prime reasons why the Red Sox have had so much trouble down through their years of frustration. For, by trying to tailor their ball clubs to Fenway Park, packing the lineup as much as possible with right-handed sluggers, they have consistently left themselves wide open for disaster on the road. Because most of those nice home runs pulled into the screen atop the Wall in Boston are just long outs everywhere else. No team can win all its games at home and lose all its games on the road and come close to winning the pennant, but the Red Sox tried. God knows they tried! For some years, they were loaded with right-handed batters who, given their choice, would never have traveled beyond Kenmore Square from one end of the season to the other.

Just why one of these right-handed pull hitting sluggers always had to be the first baseman is something I simply can't fathom. Up until recent years, I asked one general manager after another—Eddie Collins, Joe Cronin, Bucky Harris, Mike Higgins—and one manager after another—Cronin, Joe McCarthy, Steve O'Neill, Lou Boudreau, Higgins, Billy Jurges, Johnny Pesky, and Billy Herman—why the first baseman has to be a powerful right-hander, and their answers have all been substantially the same: "Because the first baseman must be a long hitter, and the best type of long hitter to use at Fenway is a big, powerful right-handed batter."

Well, there certainly have been plenty of big, powerful right-handed batters passing through Boston's dugout runway: Jimmy Foxx, Cronin (who finished his career at first base after having played most of it at short), Rudy York, Jake Jones, Walt Dropo, Dick Gernert, Norm Zauchin, Dick Stuart, George Scott, and Ken Harrelson come immediately to mind. True, the club won its only two pennants of modern times—1946 with York and 1967 with Scott—when it had a strong, right-handed hitting first baseman.

But those years just prove that a big, right-handed hitting first baseman, along with a few other sluggers hitting from either side of the plate as well as a good pitching staff, is helpful in any pennant quest. And I have no doubt that a balanced club, such as those that did win, would have done just as well with a left-handed hitting first baseman.

Two of the best first basemen in Boston since the end of World War II, the late Harry Agganis and Billy Goodman, were left-handed batters. Agganis was tall and powerful, but Goodman, the 1950 American League batting champion, was of average height and weight. So was another Red Sox first baseman—a two-time league batting leader—Pete Runnels.

Boston's two greatest hitters in modern times were Ted Williams and Carl Yastrzemski, both left-handed batters. Yastrzemski was and still is an occasional first baseman. One young man who groomed for the job was Cecil

Cooper, tall and skinny—and left-handed. But the present general manager, Dick O'Connell, is not obsessed with this passion for a big, strong, right-handed slugger at first.

"It isn't a matter of essentially having a right-handed slugging first baseman," he once told me. "But in our park we're always looking for right-handers who can hit a long ball. If one happens to be a first baseman, so much the better, because the first baseman should be a good hitter. So should the outfielders. So should the infielders. So should the catcher. So should everybody."

This sounds more reasonable than any of the arguments I've received from O'Connell's predecessors. It's very nice to have sluggers at every position, but they can't be one-way sluggers—dead pull hitters who can't do anything else at the plate. And therein lies the tale of many a Red Sox woe. They've simply had too many hitters like that.

A quick look at the parade of big right-handed first basemen gives a clue to the problem. Rudy York rounded out the most effective ball club Boston ever had—the 1946 team—but he certainly didn't lead them to that runaway pennant. If anyone, it was Ted Williams who did.

Jake Jones, who followed York, came to Boston in a man-for-man trade with the Chicago White Sox. Jones couldn't have made a more auspicious debut. On his first appearance in a Red Sox uniform, at home, he won the first game of a doubleheader with a home run over the left field fence. He then won the second with another homer to the same place.

And that was just about the end of Jake Jones. The front office feeling went from ecstasy to joy to hope to disappointment in roughly one season. A year after his day of glory, Jake had become "Popup" Jones and was finally succeeded at first base by Billy Goodman, who was neither right-handed nor powerful.

What Jake Jones had for one day, Walt Dropo had for one season. Dropo, a huge, good-natured University of Connecticut graduate, who batted right-handed and played first base, made everyone in the organization drool when he first came around. In batting practice, he hit one screaming shot after another over that chummy left field fence.

"The second coming of Foxx," the Red Sox said. "A young Rudy York. The perfect first baseman for Fenway Park. The answer to all our dreams. We'll have pennants coming out of our ears."

Dropo had a rookie season in 1950 that looked uncannily like the one Ted Williams had had in 1939. He and his teammate, Junior Stephens, shared the American League leadership in RBIs with 144. As a rookie, Williams led the league with 145. Dropo batted .338, Williams .327. Dropo hit thirty-eight home runs, Williams thirty-one.

Along with Williams and Stephens, who still holds the lifetime home-run record among American League shortstops, Dropo gave Boston one of baseball history's most murderous one-two-three punches. Because of an All-Star game injury, Williams played only the first half of the 1950 season, during which the team tore apart almost everyone who visited Fenway Park. The Red Sox brass sat contentedly back and decided that first base was one position it could forget about for the next fifteen years. Dropo, who stood nearly six feet, six inches, indeed looked the part of a star of the first magnitude.

Nobody knows precisely what went wrong. Maybe the combination of adulation, overconfidence, and the sophomore jinx was more than Dropo could handle. In any event, he had a mediocre second season in 1951. By June of 1952, however, he seemed to have regained his touch. He was leading the club with 27 RBIs, when Boston suddenly traded him to Detroit in one of the biggest player deals involving regulars ever made. Dropo, Johnny Pesky, Don Lenhardt, and a couple of others went to the Tigers for pitcher Dizzy Trout, third baseman George Kell, outfielder Hoot Evers, and shortstop Johnny Lipon.

As far as the Red Sox were concerned, the premature exit of Walt Dropo from their company finished off the second coming of Jimmy Foxx, the young Rudy York, the perfect Fenway first baseman, the answer to all their dreams, and the pennants that were expected to come out of their ears.

No right-handed hitting first baseman ever came close after that. Plenty of big ones were tried, but none left a lasting impression. Dick Gernert, the man who replaced Dropo—and, according to the brass, the reason they could afford to trade Dropo—was almost as big, but not nearly as good. Neither was Norm Zauchin, another huge right-hander of doubtful ability.

When George Scott came along in 1966, he was fresh from leading the Eastern League in practically every hitting and fielding category, not as a first baseman but as a third baseman. The Red Sox moved him to first to make room for Joe Foy, another third baseman, and for two years Scott seemed to be a combination of Foxx and Dropo. As a rookie in 1966 he hit twenty-seven homers and batted in ninety runs, and he hit .303 on the 1967 pennant-winning club. He then went into a steady decline, alternated between first and third for a few years, and finally was traded to Milwaukee in another multi-player deal in October of 1971.

But Scott was the first big right-handed slugging first baseman to land in Boston by accident. All the others were dug up purposely, because for years the scouts had instructions to look for guys like that. Scott was signed because he happened to be a good ballplayer who could hit. That he also could adjust well to first base was just a happy accident.

Once the Red Sox had Scott, you might have thought they not only would hail him as the second coming of Walt Dropo at least, but would keep him on first base. Perhaps earlier Red Sox executives would have. But for two reasons, Scott was never a full-time first baseman after 1967. One reason was Joe Foy's collapse. After a fine season at third in 1967, he fell apart, so Scott was moved into his place and Ken Harrelson brought in from right field to play first base, where he was much more at home. Harrelson, too, fitted the old image of the ideal first baseman, since he was a big right-handed batter who could hit with power.

The other reason Scott played first base only sporadically after 1967 was his own collapse at the plate, and that was as much the Wall's fault as Scott's. Having sniffed the sweet smell of the Wall for two years, Scott couldn't resist the temptation to aim for it every time he came to bat. No matter where the pitches came; they could be high, low, wide, tight, or over Scott's head. He was not fussy about what he swung at. The result was disaster. Scott hit three homers, drove in twenty-five runs, and batted .171 in 124 ball games in 1968 and never had another season like 1967. By the time the Red Sox traded him to Milwaukee after the 1971 season ended, the most promising twenty-three-year-old first baseman since Dropo had been transformed into a twenty-seven-year-old victim of too many bad pitches.

When Dick Williams, perhaps the best manager the Red Sox ever had, publicly declared that "talking to Scott is like talking to the wall," he didn't mean Fenway's left field fence. Williams made one of his few mistakes as manager by giving Scott the ice when he most needed encouragement. But nobody could have done much for Scott by the middle of that disastrous 1968 season. He had already been done in by the Wall.

If it weren't for the Wall, Scott might still be in Boston. The Wall embraced Scott like a long-lost brother in 1966 and hugged him even more tightly in 1967. The Wall was his friend. But when he tried to get chummy with the Wall, it turned its back on him.

Scott was not the Wall's first victim, nor will he be the last. The front office executives were victims of the Wall from Eddie Collins' time to Dick O'Connell's. O'Connell was the first general manager in memory who didn't try to tailor the ball club to the Wall and who worried as much about the team on the road as at home.

Not that he wasn't aware of the Wall. Nor did he go the other way and deliberately look for left-handed first basemen or hitters. He simply gave orders to the farm personnel to sign promising ballplayers, regardless of where they played or which side of the plate they batted from.

"We need balance," O'Connell once said. "Every club needs it. But most clubs play half their games in ball parks that don't favor either right-handers or left-handers. We play half our games in a park that definitely favors right-handers. So we're not going to stick our noses up at long-hitting right-handers. That would be insane.

"On the other hand, the whole modern history of the Red Sox shows excellent home and poor road records. The 1946 team, maybe the best we ever had because it was a combination of great hitters, great pitchers, and good fielders, didn't win the pennant on the road. Because of its tremendous right-handed power, it was simply unbeatable at home.

"But," O'Connell butted, "how often do you get a team with such a top-heavy home record that it can get by with only a fair record on the road? We can't afford to pack our lineup with right-handed batters because you must do well on the road to win."

O'Connell was right about the 1946 team. Except for Ted Williams and Johnny Pesky, it was loaded with right-handers who had the range of the Wall. York, Doerr, Higgins, and DiMaggio got plenty of homers that cleared it and dozens of lesser hits that caromed off it. Add to that the drives Williams hit to center, some of which ended up in the screen or the bleachers, while others bounced off the Wall to the left of center, and it is easy to see what an important part the Wall played in that 1946 team.

Backed by outstanding pitching, the 1946 Red Sox won 104 games and lost 50. On the road their record was nothing remarkable: they won 43 games and lost 34. But at home they were virtually unbeatable, since they won 61 and lost 16. The only team in history to top that record in a 154-game season were the 1932 New York Yankees, who won 62 and lost 15 at home.

Thus, it would seem that any team which could win at least 61 out of 77 games at home would be sure pennant winners, as the 1946 Red Sox and 1932 Yankees were. But the 1949 Red Sox also won 61 and lost only 16 games at home, yet didn't win the pennant. They blew up on the last weekend of the season, when they went into New York a game in front with two to play and lost both.

The difference was that the 1946 team was 43–34 on the road, but the 1949 club won only 35 and lost 42 away from the cozy confines of Fenway Park. No team in major-league history has had such success at home and such disaster abroad. In order to lose the 1949 pennant, the Red Sox *had* to be terrible on the road—and they were.

The other modern Red Sox winners, the 1967 team, was packed with right-handed hitters, but it was altogether different from the 1946 team. For starters, the pitching, with Jim Lonborg the only twenty-game winner (he won twenty-two) was nowhere near as good. And although Ted Williams was the 1946 star, he didn't stand head and shoulders over everyone else, as Carl Yastrzemski did in 1967. The two left-handed superstars produced astonishingly similar records in those pennant years. Williams had 38 homers, 123 RBIs and hit .342, without leading the league in any of those categories. Yastrzemski had 44 homers, 121 RBIs, hit .326, and won the Triple Crown.

Furthermore, the right-handed 1946 Red Sox took full

advantage of the Wall, which the right-handed 1967 team didn't. Scott and Petrocelli, who hit nineteen and seventeen homers respectively, hit nearly as many on the road as at home. But Mike Andrews and Joe Foy weren't long ball hitters even at Fenway. Neither was Elston Howard, who joined the club early in August and totaled only four homers for the year. Ken Harrelson came to the Red Sox too late to do much. His twelve round-trippers that year were mostly at Kansas City. And Reggie Smith, who hit fifteen homers in 1967, wasn't just a right-handed batter, but a switch hitter with almost as much power from one side of the plate as the other.

This 1967 team didn't come near dominating the league at home. Their pennant was won with similar records at home and on the road: 49–32 in Fenway Park and 43–38 elsewhere. Perhaps the most significant difference was that while the 1946 team walked away with the pennant, the 1967 team won it on the last day of the season.

What these statistics prove is that the 1946 club was primarily built around the Wall, and the 1967 club wasn't. They also prove that the 1967 team was even better balanced than the 1946 team, since they did almost as well on the road as at home. Yet, man for man and figure for figure, there is no comparison between the two teams; the 1946 club was far and away superior, and the difference was not just pitching.

Compare the teams position by position. York at first base couldn't hold Scott's glove, but he was a much more consistent hitter. Doerr at second was better than Andrews, and Higgins was better than Foy at third. The only infield superiority the 1967 team had was at short, where Petrocelli topped Pesky, and on the bench, where Jerry Adair had an amazing season, filling in wherever he was needed.

Great as he was in 1967, even Yastrzemski would be the first to admit that Williams, his 1946 counterpart in left field, was the better ballplayer in all respects except team leadership, at which the 1967 Yastrzemski was in a class by himself. Dom DiMaggio was a better all around center fielder than Reggie Smith. Only in right was the 1967 team clearly better in the outfield. While the 1946 club floundered around with three or four right fielders of doubtful quality, the 1967 team started the season with Tony Conigliaro. After he was hurt, his replacements, Jose Tartabull, Ken Harrelson, and George Thomas, were all better than anyone on the 1946 team. Hal Wagner of the 1946 team was a better catcher than any of the 1967 catchers until Elston Howard arrived on the scene. And the 1946 pitching was far superior. Except for Lonborg, the 1967 staff was actually below average.

Yet both teams won pennants. Why?

Because the 1946 team took full advantage of the Wall? Maybe. But pre-World War II Red Sox teams, with slugging right-handed hitters like Foxx, Cronin, Doerr, DiMaggio, and Jim Tabor, took full advantage of the Wall and didn't win a pennant. And the 1967 team did a pretty good job of ignoring the Wall and did.

The Wall wasn't the answer, not by itself. It helped in 1946 because the team also had great pitching. But the Wall was a lesser factor in 1967, because the club's inspirational leader and top hitter, Carl Yastrzemski, was a left-handed batter who hit or cleared it occasionally, but got most of his Fenway Park drives hitting straightaway or pulling to right field.

The answer really lies in the caliber of the rest of the league. The 1946 team won by such a wide margin because it overpowered everyone else while enjoying phenomenal pitching. The 1967 team won by such a narrow margin because, although it had only one first-class pitcher, it was shrewdly managed and had confidence, guts, togetherness, and Carl Yastrzemski. It had to fight off challenges from the Twins, the Tigers, and the White Sox until the middle of the last week of the season, and when the White Sox dropped out, from the other two teams until the last day.

If the 1967 team had tried to feed off the Wall, they wouldn't have won the pennant. The Wall could have killed the 1967 team, just as it had so many other Red Sox teams, if Manager Dick Williams had allowed it to. But Williams played tight baseball, with heavy emphasis on stretching hits, bunting, the hit-and-run, stealing, and generally playing for a run or two. Yastrzemski was the big hitter and got the big hits, but even he occasionally had orders from Dick Williams to play for a run instead of a cluster of them.

With all that right-handed power and Ted Williams, too, the 1946 team used the Wall to play for big innings. When the club played at home, they crushed the opposition with clusters of runs rattling off and over the Wall. That may have been the way to score runs, but if it had been the way to win pennants, the Red Sox would have won half a dozen or more instead of only two from 1938 on.

Of course, you can't blame the Wall for everything. But when you try to find out what's been wrong with the Red

Sox all these years, you realize that it must be partly responsible. For one thing, too many of the club's top executives tried to build teams around the Wall.

The problem was not simply that right-handed power
hitters could use the Wall at home and couldn't on the
road. The real problem was that the Wall affected everybody's swing. Even intelligent right-handed batters who
knew they would never be power hitters anywhere but
Fenway Park were victimized. At home they unconsciously
got into the habit of swinging for the Wall. Then, when
they left Boston, it took them half a road trip to get out of
the habit. In their regular straightaway swinging grooves
they managed very nicely until they got home. There with
the Wall beckoning again, they were mesmerized into going for it.

Thus, up until recently every right-handed batter who
played for the Red Sox thought he was a slugger because
he was rattling hits off the Wall and occasionally smack-
ing homers over it. But most were not sluggers and
wouldn't have been considered such if they hadn't been
playing half their games at Fenway.

Even visiting right-handers, banjo hitters as well as legitimate sluggers, got into trouble because of the Wall. Every
team that visits Boston, even for a day or two, is bitten by
the same bug that infected Red Sox right-handers for so
long. More than one visiting manager has looked at the
Wall before a game and said, "I hate that damn thing. I've
got good hitters who take one look at it and go crazy. They
change their stance, their swing, their whole philosophy of
hitting just to take advantage of a fence they don't see a
dozen times a year."

And then the same manager, after complaining in this way, will sigh and say, "But how can I blame them? I was just as bad when I came here as a player. They ought to put a lighthouse on that thing to warn right-handed spray hitters to stay the hell away from it."

Truly, the Wall is baseball's Lorelei, luring all hitters with its beauty and apparent accessibility and ruining many when they fall for it. It is really good for only one type of hitter—the big man who pulls to left field no matter where he plays. Joe DiMaggio loved it. So did Mickey Mantle, when a southpaw was pitching against the Yankees, as did Frank Robinson when he was at Baltimore. So, too, does Harmon Killebrew of the Twins. And Sal Bando of the A's. And Bill Freehan and Willie Horton of the Tigers. And Frank Howard who once came into town with the Washington Senators and nearly ripped the screen above the Wall apart. And Bill Melton of the White Sox, the American League's home-run king in 1971. It was Tony Conigliaro's favorite target before his career was ruined in 1967 by a fast ball that hit him in the face.

But through the years the Wall has actually helped the Red Sox more defensively than offensively. Although there have been a few others, only two men have played Boston's left field for most of the time since 1939—Ted Williams and Carl Yastrzemski. Because both were such outstanding hitters, neither got the credit he deserved for his defensive play off the Wall.

Williams was good, Yastrzemski superb. Both studied the Wall until they knew every little nick, every possible carom, and where to station themselves to get a ball bouncing off it. Yastrzemski, more agile and with a better arm, knew the Wall so well he could play tricks on hitters. Whenever a ball was hit to left, he could tell almost exactly where it would hit or if it would clear the fence. If it were headed for the screen he did nothing, because there was nothing he could do—it was gone for a home run. But if the ball was going to carom off the fence out of his reach, with a man on base, Yastrzemski was marvelous at faking a catch he knew he couldn't make, standing at the place where he was sure the ball would come down.

Invariably, even experienced ballplayers were fooled into staying close enough to the bag to get back in case Yastrzemski made the catch. When he didn't, they would scramble to make it to the next base. Had they anticipated the ball hitting the Wall up high, at least one extra base would have been easy.

For thirty-five years, the longest singles in the big leagues have been hit to left field at Fenway Park. Sometimes Yastrzemski, with his rifle arm, has actually forced a man at second, robbing the batter of a hit because the man on first was afraid to advance. Although Williams wasn't as good as Yastrzemski at faking catches, he too had a rifle arm, which kept many an extra-base hit down to a single. No visiting left fielder has ever learned the knack of playing the Wall as well as the two Red Sox superstars.

Because of the Wall and the way Boston fielders play it, anything going to left is usually either a single or a home run, if hit by the opposition. Experienced line-drive right-handed batters don't like the Wall because they can seldom clear it, and if they don't, all they can expect is a single. In most major-league ball parks, it is possible to hit a line-drive home run to left, but Boston's high fence in left prohibits this. But by the same token, Red Sox players can often convert line drives to left into doubles or even triples, because their rivals are not as familiar with the fence. In this way, the Wall does offer an advantage to Boston ballplayers.

After all these years, the jury may still be out on the question of that Fenway Park wall, but I have long since come to the conclusion that it has done more harm than good. It would be a mistake not to consider the Wall as a factor in what's wrong with the Red Sox. And because of it, Boston has made more than its share of stupid deals.

Any right-handed ballplayer who in one visit hits more than one homer into or over the left field screen has been a prime candidate for membership in the Red Sox club. I particularly remember a St. Louis Browns catcher, Les Moss, who once came into Boston and beat a tattoo off and over the Wall in a four-game series. Immediately the press began speculating on how long it would be before the Red Sox would trade for him. While denying any such possibility, the front office began dickering with Bill Veeck, who then ran the Browns, and finally completed a deal during the winter. The terms of the trade were cash, a couple of ballplayers on the spot, and "one to be named later." As soon as he was in a Red Sox uniform, the catcher's bat went cold. He might have hit a few off the Wall and perhaps even a homer or two, but in an entire season Moss failed to get as many hits out of it as he had during that one four-game series. When the season ended, he became the player "to be named later." The Red Sox sent him back to the Browns, the only time in history a traded player was used as partial payment for himself.

When he got Moss back, Veeck announced, "I'll rent the Red Sox any player they want for $100,000 a year."

On the other hand, catcher Birdie Tebbetts, who went to the Red Sox from Detroit, blossomed into a slugger because of the Wall. Since he came from New Hampshire, where his family still lived, Tebbetts was delighted to be in Boston anyhow. The Wall just added frosting to his cake.

Fenway Park without the Wall would seem like Mount Rushmore without its granite faces, though it has cost the Red Sox plenty. Yet the familiar fence remains as much a part of Boston's baseball scene as all the remembrances of things past—many of which it has inspired. And who would have things any other way?

CHAPTER 3

Tom Yawkey

It is impossible to understand the modern Red Sox without trying to understand the character of Tom Yawkey, the man who made them what they are today. Because of his passion for privacy, his general refusal to appear in public, the manner in which he drops virtually out of sight every year from October to May, and his reluctance to talk about himself, this isn't easy.

Although always courteous, a gentleman from the top of his closely-cropped hair to the shiny toes of his shoes, an easy and often willing interview as long as the subject is baseball, Yawkey is in many ways an enigma. Self-effacing, impatient with those who try to praise him, proud of his heritage as a member of one of America's oldest and most substantial families, totally generous as long as his generosity isn't publicized, and a jealous guardian of all his affairs that do not relate to baseball, he seems to turn himself on and off at will. Some of his best friends are the little people who hang around the ball park—groundskeepers, ushers, peanut vendors, and the youngsters.

He rarely misses a Red Sox home game, which he views from his private box atop the grandstand at the same level as the press box. In an adjoining box is Mrs. Yawkey, a charming woman with the same type of shyness that characterizes her husband. One or the other may have guests, but a good part of the time each is alone, talking from time to time around the glass partition that separates them. No one, not even a front-office executive, enters Yawkey's box without an invitation. If he wants anything or anyone, he asks—never orders or demands—on his own phone. During a game, even when he is deep in conversation, his eyes are constantly on the field. Although Yawkey never makes appointments when a ball game is in progress, he sees people on the spur of the moment if the subject is important and relates to baseball.

He has a New York office, T. A. Yawkey Enterprises, where all his nonbaseball interests are handled. He himself is rarely there. He once kept a New York apartment, but doesn't now. When not in Boston he is almost always at his home, an island off the coast of South Carolina, not far from Georgetown. He lives simply, dresses casually, and spends a great deal of time hunting, for which he had a passion in his younger days and still enjoys. His Boston home, as it has been since he bought the Red Sox, is a hotel suite.

As a general rule, Yawkey cannot be reached directly by phone, even at Fenway Park. Unless the caller is known or a secretary has been told to put somebody through, he takes no calls. However, he is told of all calls, and he will acknowledge a message either through a secretary or by arranging an appointment with the caller if he feels there is reason to do so.

Although Yawkey's interest in baseball has sometimes flagged, it is intense most of the time. The game is in his blood. He was, in a sense, born to it. His uncle, William H. Yawkey, who adopted him as a baby, owned the Detroit Tigers from 1904 through 1907. The Yawkey family is still deeply involved in the interests, primarily mining and lumber, on which the original family fortune was built. But their name was never a household word until Tom bought the Red Sox, and his long ownership of the team has resulted in more publicity than anything anyone else in the family ever did.

Yawkey has for years been vice-president of the American League, and he still swings a good deal of clout in league affairs, although not as much as he once did. Illness in the early and mid-sixties slowed him considerably, and that illness, rather than the club's failure to get anywhere in that period, was the cause of Yawkey's only known withdrawal from the game.

His best cure was the 1967 pennant, a surprise to him as much as to everyone else. The 1966 Red Sox were a ninth-place club, and their comeback was duplicated only by the New York Mets, who won the 1969 pennant after finishing ninth in 1968. From 1967 to this writing, Yawkey's enthusiasm for baseball has been as strong as ever.

Whether the team is at home or on the road, Yawkey is at Fenway Park almost every day during the baseball season, after the first month. He listens to road games on the radio or watches them on television while keeping track of the other major-league teams on his private baseball ticker, which gives vital statistics and inning-by-inning results as they happen. Although his primary interest is, naturally, the American League, he keeps close tabs on the National, and all the minor-league information that comes over the ticker as well.

The millions Yawkey has invested in the Red Sox he considers money well spent, for he feels he has got it all back in pleasure and thrills. His reputation for generosity is well-earned and not confined to ballplayers' salaries. He has contributed heavily to many charities, including the Jimmy Fund, which supplied the money to build a children's cancer research wing of the Boston Children's Hospital. Much of the money is raised through the Red Sox, who run intensive campaigns each year for this cause.

Little is known of Yawkey's personal life, which is the way he wants it. The only time I've ever heard him refer to family other than his wife was in 1965, when, because he seemed to be losing interest in the Red Sox, there was a good deal of talk about his selling the team.

"I would never sell it," he said at the time. "It is one thing I want to leave to my heirs—I have nieces and nephews, you know. What they do with the club will be up to them."

The Red Sox franchise is probably the only possession of Yawkey's that he has bought on his own, without benefit of family business advisors. Practically everything else he owns is thought to be part of the massive family interests handled through his New York office. He seems to neither know nor care much about these affairs, for he is utterly wrapped up in baseball. He is justifiably proud of having built up the ball club from a faltering loser in every way to a strong, healthy organization which has become a rousing financial success.

The Red Sox are his own, nobody else's, and his affection for them is like that of a parent for a child. His interest itself tends to be childlike, and his enthusiasm is more that of an intense fan than an owner. He talks about the team just like a fan except in one respect—no matter how bad a blunder is made, he never criticizes either the team or any individual member of it. He can stand anything but disloyalty. The Red Sox have unloaded several good ball players for saying something critical about them in the off-season. When this happens, Yawkey simply gives the order, "Get rid of him," and the front office gets rid of him, no matter what the effect on the team.

This happened in the case of Birdie Tebbetts, an outspoken catcher who blamed a couple of pitchers for the loss of the 1948 and 1949 pennants. In talks on the banquet circuit, Tebbetts referred to young pitchers who, he implied, choked up when they were needed most. Yawkey didn't care whether Tebbetts was right or wrong. The fact that he criticized *anyone* on the ball club, in his mind, constituted disloyalty.

When the Red Sox couldn't make a deal for Tebbetts, they sold him to Cleveland—and left themselves without a catcher of major-league experience. Fortunately, Sammy White came up as a rookie the next year. If he hadn't, they would have had to trade for an adequate receiver.

However, the Tebbetts case was extreme. Yawkey usually had a better reason than that for dealing off a ballplayer. Just how much he runs the team and how much he leaves up to his general managers has long been a question.

In the beginning it wasn't. Eddie Collins ran the club with an iron hand. He told Yawkey what he was doing and why, but the decisions were his.

The rise of the Red Sox under Yawkey's ownership—thanks to Collins's perspicacity and, of course, Yawkey's money—was spectacular. The club was last in 1932, just before Yawkey bought them, and second by 1938. In the twenty-five years between 1933 and 1958, Boston finished out of the first division in the eight-club American League only five times, twice during World War II. During the same period they won one pennant and were second six times, all but once to the pennant-winning New York Yankees.

New England and the Maritime Provinces are full of Red Sox fans who think Yawkey has done the club more harm than good. This is absurd. After saving them from certain bankruptcy, he built them into almost perpetual contenders. His worst mistakes stemmed from kindness, decency, and generosity; he is the last of the sentimental baseball owners. The price he has paid for this sentimentality can't possibly be measured, but I'll venture to say that a tougher Tom Yawkey would have meant several more pennants.

His loyalty extends well beyond the ball field. He has stayed with more than one key executive too long, and has let too many of his front office appointments be ruled by personal feelings. All his general managers during the period between Collins and Dick O'Connell—both tough, hard-shelled, practical businessmen—had few qualifications beyond their personal friendship with Yawkey.

Joe Cronin, a great ballplayer who earned his membership in baseball's Hall of Fame on the field, was a poor general manager and is now simply a figurehead as president of the American League. Yawkey kept Cronin in the front office from 1948 through 1959, a period when the club won no pennants. A warm, friendly man, Cronin shared one of Yawkey's worst faults—he didn't know how to fire anyone. The result was a dreadful clutter of deadwood at almost all levels. When Cronin left for the American League presidency, which Yawkey was instrumental in getting for him, the Red Sox were on a decline in which they finished seventh twice, eighth twice, and ninth twice before winning the 1967 pennant.

Cronin's successor, Bucky Harris, was another example of Yawkey's misplaced loyalty. Harris actually got into the Red Sox organization because of a promise twenty-two years earlier by Yawkey, who was personally very fond of him. For that matter, so was just about everyone who knew him, for Harris, like Cronin, had far more warmth and charm than executive ability.

Harris was the first manager the Red Sox hired after Yawkey bought the team. He ran the club in 1934, succeeding the 1933 manager, Marty McManus, who was a holdover from the previous regime. Then in 1935 Yawkey bought Joe Cronin, who had managed the Washington Senators to the 1933 pennant, to be the Red Sox playermanager. But before completing the deal, Yawkey made sure that the Washington owner, Clark Griffith, would rehire Harris, who had already had the job once, as the Senator's manager. And when Harris left Boston to make room for Cronin, Yawkey assured him the Red Sox would always have a job for him if he needed one.

Harris held him to that promise when the Tigers fired him as manager in 1956. Yawkey, who had maintained a close personal relationship with Harris through the years, unhesitatingly hired him as a special front office assistant and superscout. He could have—and undoubtedly should have—stopped there. But he then proceeded to name Harris general manager when Cronin left. It was a ghastly mistake. Harris, a good field manager in his time, had less to offer than Cronin out front.

Sentimentality has always been Yawkey's biggest weakness. Too many of his key appointments were dictated by his heart, not his head. His loyalty to the late Mike Higgins, who twice served as manager and was O'Connell's immediate predecessor as general manager, cost Yawkey years of progress in his everlasting quest for pennants.

While Yawkey, to my knowledge, never knowingly hurt a soul, one of the men he admired most, Ted Williams, was the only baseball figure I'm aware of who ever hurt him. Yawkey treated Williams like an adored kid brother. He backed Ted so wholeheartedly in the long feud with the press that he himself was battling the writers just for their handling of Williams. He gave Williams deferred contracts, paying him huge sums for doing nothing but helping out with young hitters for a few weeks every spring. And for years, Williams gave him value for value in return. What Williams did for Carl Yastrzemski alone was worth all the money Yawkey paid him.

But Yawkey didn't ever consider Williams an employee. Nor did he care whether he would earn the deferred salaries or not. Tom Yawkey simply asked one thing of Williams—loyalty. And until 1967 he got it.

When Dick Williams took the Red Sox to the 1967 pennant, Yawkey was truly in seventh heaven. Whether or not he knew it, however, the two Williamses, Dick and Ted, didn't get along at all. At spring training in 1967, Ted sneered at Dick's managerial methods, while Dick made it evident that he would be just as pleased if Ted would stay the hell away from his training camp. Ted left and never returned in any Red Sox capacity.

Not until the 1967 World Series did I hear Ted Williams's name mentioned again around Fenway Park. Just before the first game, I ran into Yawkey on his way to his private box.

"Have you seen Ted?" I asked.

"He'll be here," Yawkey said. "I know he'll be here."

I didn't see Yawkey again until the seventh game, which was also played in Boston. Once again, we met on the Fenway Park roof.

"Did he come?" I asked.

"The big guy?" Yawkey replied. There was the trace of a frown on his face, as though something was hurting. Then he brightened, smiled, and said, "The big guy will come for this game. You watch. He'll be here." But Williams wasn't there for that game either. I was told later that he wired congratulations, but so did about a million other people.

I truly think Yawkey was bothered more by Ted's thoughtlessness in not even trying to reach him by phone than by the loss of the Series to the Cardinals. Yet I am sure that when Williams made later trips to Boston as manager of the Washington Senators (or Texas Rangers after they moved), he and Yawkey got together. It would

be characteristic of Yawkey to act toward Williams as if
nothing had happened, but there is no question that at the
time of the Series he was keenly hurt.

Still they remained friends despite the events of October,
1967. And before taking the job of managing the Washing-
ton-Texas club, Williams talked several times to Yawkey
on the phone. In fact, he virtually asked for—and got—
Yawkey's blessing. Ted could have become the Red Sox
manager any time up to 1967, but he had no desire to return to baseball in Boston after retiring as a player. While
it was an accepted fact that his unpleasant relations with
the local press were a strong factor in this, far more important to Williams was a chance to become part owner
of a ball club.

This was the prime lure that attracted Ted into the Wash-
ington-Texas orbit. When Bob Short offered him the job of
manager while the club was still in Washington, he also
offered him stock in the team, along with an astronomical
salary. Williams could have had the same salary from
Yawkey, but stock in the Red Sox was something else
again.

Yawkey is the sole owner of the Red Sox, and I'm sure
he will remain so as long as he lives. He would never give
up a share to anyone, not even a pre-1967 Ted Williams.
I confirmed this in a talk with Yawkey in the summer of
1972.

"If you were told you would have to give up all your
possessions one by one," I asked, "what is the last thing
you would let go?"

Yawkey speaks rapidly, often biting off his words while
letting clouds of cigarette smoke obscure his face. Except

for frequent "Goddamns," he uses almost no profanity. His skin, which looks as fragile as papyrus, is generously but not heavily lined. There are no deep wrinkles, just scores of tiny ones, which accentuate the papyrus effect. When he smiles, these wrinkles don't deepen. They simply spread.

He smiled, smoked furiously for a moment, then said, "It might be my place in South Carolina, or it might be the Red Sox." He paused, smiled again, and added, "It would be a tie—at least, I *think* it would be a tie. I love my home. The air is so clean and clear. I used to hunt ducks there, but I've made it a duck and goose sanctuary. I'd find it difficult to give that up.

"But I'd find it just as hard to give up the Red Sox. They are so much a part of me, a part of my life. I shall have owned them forty years next February [1973]. I came into my inheritance at thirty—that was 1933—and I had to wait until then to have the money to buy the club and do the things I wanted to with it."

He shook his head, crushed out the cigarette, and the lines in his face increased as he smiled again.

"It's a tough question," he said. "I can't answer it. I think it would be a tie."

A tie. The Red Sox or his home. He loves them both equally. This may reflect a characteristic of Yawkey that must go back many years, perhaps all the way to his childhood. I suspect he was something of a poor little rich boy, who had everything, yet nothing that was really his and his alone. Perhaps the Red Sox and his South Carolina island are the only possessions which belong *completely* to him. No one gave or bequeathed or left him either. They are *his*.

It must mean a great deal to Yawkey to know that the Red Sox, always popular in the northeast, have become a New England institution under his stewardship. From the day he bought the club four months after it finished in the American League cellar in 1932, right up to the present, it has been all his to do with as he pleased, when he pleased, without advice from anyone but people he had selected himself.

By his thirtieth birthday, Yawkey wasn't just a baseball fan. He had a passion for the game, an admiration for everyone in it, as well as an unquenchable thirst to make a career of his own by operating a big-league franchise.

"Perhaps some people think I have wasted my life," he told me, in his staccato, runaway speech. "I can't help that. I was always taught to help others, that those of us fortunate enough to be born with material abundance should do what we can for those who are not. I do what I can. In forty years I have tried to provide jobs, to give pleasure, to treat human beings like human beings."

"Have you ever had reason to regret it?" I asked. "Have people ever disappointed you?"

He reached for a cigarette from a silver box on his desk. As he lit it—with a match—I looked up at a picture of President Eisenhower, personally autographed to him, on the wall over his head. My eyes wandered to another picture, of the handsome, young, dark-haired Red Sox owner at thirty. Beside him sat the stern, spare, jug-eared Eddie Collins, the general manager he had just appointed—one of the first general managers in major-league baseball.

"I have never had reason to regret it." Yawkey was speaking more slowly, weighing his words. "As for disappointments in people—yes, I've had them."

He paused, and I thought of Ted Williams and the 1967 World Series, but I couldn't mention that incident. Yawkey is a proud man, and it would have bothered him to know I remembered our brief meetings then and his deep sense of hurt at that time.

Instead, I asked, "Have those disappointments changed your attitude about people?"

He shook his head, and his words ran together as he said, "It's hard to change character traits. If you let disappointments sour you, you'll change your whole philosophy, and I could never change mine. Haven't. Won't. The man who lets disappointments change his thinking about people couldn't have had that thinking very deeply ingrained in him, as mine was in me. No. Disappointments haven't changed me. What I learned growing up is more important to me than anything anyone could have done to me after I put my principles into practice."

By the time Yawkey actually bought the ball club for something in the neighborhood of a million dollars—one hell of a lot of money in 1933—he was already planning to hire Collins as general manager. His admiration for Collins was not based just on Collins's fantastic baseball record. Yawkey had spent eight years at the Irving School in Tarrytown, New York, before entering Yale. Years before Yawkey's time, Collins had prepared for Columbia at this same Irving School, which is no longer in existence.

"One of the most coveted prizes at the school was the Edward T. Collins Medal for the best scholar-athlete,"

Yawkey told me. "My roommate, Alan McMartin, who later played on the Canadian Davis Cup tennis team, won it, and I was the runner-up. So, you see, the fact that Eddie Collins was a great, great baseball player was not his only credential in my mind when I asked permission of Connie Mack to talk to him about becoming my general manager."

Collins was a natural for the job. Perhaps the finest second baseman who ever lived, he had had the longest span of major-league playing activity of any man in history— twenty-five years, beginning in 1906. He had a reputation for integrity and intelligence, a combination Yawkey would have admired in anyone, not just a former ball-player. It is no exaggeration to say that Collins might well be the smartest ballplayer the major leagues have ever known. He won his 1906 Columbia degree in the classroom, not the ball field, at a time when few major leaguers made it through high school.

His reputation for integrity was so spotless that the gamblers who paid eight White Sox players for throwing the 1919 World Series to the Cincinnati Reds (they were forever after known as the Black Sox) didn't dare approach Collins. He was one of the few White Sox regulars not involved in the most famous sports scandal in history. On top of which, Collins knew as much baseball as anyone in the game, had once been Chicago's player-manager, and, because he started and finished his career with the Athletics, had spent many years at the feet of baseball's great master, Connie Mack.

When Yawkey hired Collins as the first Red Sox general manager the young owner gave him carte blanche to do whatever he felt necessary to build a winning ball club.

The fact that Collins happened to be Connie Mack's favorite ballplayer—he had been an Athletics' coach when Yawkey hired him—was helpful. Mack was in the process of breaking up a championship team for the second time, a financial necessity, since Philadelphia baseball fans had a strange habit of getting bored with winners. The only way Mack could keep going was to sell off his stars, and at the time Yawkey purchased the Red Sox, Mack still had plenty of stars left to sell.

Obviously, the Philadelphia owner-manager had to split them up. He sent a few to the White Sox, including Jimmy Dykes, who became manager. A few others went to Detroit, including Mickey Cochrane, who became manager there. The remaining standouts, including Lefty Grove and Jimmy Foxx, were sold to the Red Sox. Eventually, Collins had on the Boston payroll seven of the Philadelphia participants in the 1931 World Series, Mack's last of three straight winning teams.

It was Collins who advised Yawkey to buy Joe Cronin from Washington for that record quarter-million price (plus one ballplayer) in time to manage and play shortstop for the 1935 team. It was Collins who suggested acquiring Wes Ferrell, the terrible-tempered but highly efficient pitcher from Cleveland, and his disciplined catcher brother, Rick, from St. Louis. Collins went to San Diego to look at a highly touted shortstop, George Myatt, and came back with a kid second baseman named Bobby Doerr and an option to buy Ted Williams, a promising schoolboy outfielder, who was already committed to the San Diego club. Collins never did recommend Myatt, who later had several mediocre years in the majors before becoming a coach, although

he starred at San Diego the first day Collins saw him, while
Doerr was making four errors at second base—and Williams was still in high school.

With Yawkey supplying the money and Collins the
know-how, the Red Sox were pennant contenders within
five years. Those may well have been the happiest years of
Yawkey's life. Literally wallowing in baseball, with a Hall-
of-Fame second baseman as constant companion, advisor,
and father figure, as well as some of the outstanding stars
of that time for pals, Yawkey lived in a fan's paradise. His
open admiration for his own ballplayers and executives was
returned tenfold. The men whose names were known
wherever baseball was played hero-worshiped Yawkey as
much as he worshiped them. He paid them well, invited
them to his winter home to hunt and to his summer quarters for parties, and mingled with them on the ball field
and in the locker room. Everybody was happy.

Except the team did not win any pennants. At first, Red
Sox fans were ecstatic over the sudden change in the fortunes of their favorites. The ball club had no trouble with
the press because, although there were more newspapers
then, there were fewer writers, and they all cooperated
with the ball club. This was perfectly natural; Yawkey was
always available for interviews, the press had plenty to
write about, and there was a certain excitement to being
in on the rebuilding of a major-league club.

The second-place finish in 1938 brought nothing but
praise from fans and press alike. Even the 1939 second-
place finish (both to the Yankees) failed to bother anyone.
But this was Ted Williams's rookie year, and because of
him, some writers refused to go along with the idea that

God was in His heaven and all was right with the Red Sox.

Here Yawkey made an important mistake, dictated by his adoration of ballplayers. He could have stopped the blossoming feud between Williams and the press by letting Williams know that he had asked for much of the grief he got from writers like Dave Egan and Duke Lake. Instead, Yawkey, apparently resenting any criticism from the press after all he had done to build up the team, took Williams' side and sowed a bit of trouble all his own.

This spawned a war, not just between Yawkey and the critical writers, but among the writers themselves. The older ones who had watched the Red Sox improve from the beginning of the new regime took Yawkey's side. While the young Turks of the press corps, who had taken the side of his critics after Williams began acting up, now started putting the slug on the club in general and Yawkey in particular.

Thus the battle lines were drawn, and gradually Yawkey was transformed in the minds of some fans from hero to villain. While this was thoroughly unfair to him, he had asked for it by not admonishing Williams in the first place. On the other hand, an unbiased observer might say, "Since when is the owner of the team a cop? Where were the manager—Cronin—and the general manager—Collins?"

Where Collins stood, I'm not absolutely sure, but I do know that Cronin, who was still playing in those days, tried to discipline Williams. Cronin, in fact, was responsible for Williams' being sent to the minors in 1938. Besides being a good move, since Williams needed that extra year in Class Triple A ball, it was necessary. Williams had acted like a bush leaguer on the way north, so Cronin sent him down to teach him a lesson.

That time Yawkey backed Cronin up. But when Cronin tried to discipline Williams after he landed with the Red Sox to stay, Yawkey, or perhaps it was Collins, either rescinded Cronin's actions or refused to announce them.

While Yawkey may not have been directly responsible for all this nonsense, who else could be blamed? A rookie ballplayer used profanity—loud and clearly—yelling at paying customers. A rookie ballplayer refused to tip his cap in response to cheers. A simple courtesy. His manager had chastised, possibly fined him. Yet the ballplayer continued to swear at fans and to snub them, and the ball club apparently condoned it.

Whatever Cronin became later, in those days he was a big leaguer in all respects. He had the courage of his convictions, the guts to tell a smart-aleck rookie off, and he intended to keep that rookie under control. Somebody above him undermined him in these moves, either Yawkey or Collins. Knowing Collins, a tough-minded, no-nonsense executive whose devotion to Yawkey was exceeded only by his devotion to baseball, it doesn't seem possible that he would have excused Williams' actions any more than Egan or Lake did. That leaves only Yawkey, who saw in Williams a potentially superb ballplayer; not a bitter, spoiled kid, but a young hero to worship; not a potential storm center, but a hitter who would leave a permanent mark of excellence on the sporting world's firmament; not a naughty boy who at that time badly needed a swift kick and a stiff fine.

Nobody could have played better baseball than Williams did in the years to follow. But his personality went astray at the crossroads. And there is every reason to believe that it was Yawkey who let him take the wrong turn. The right turn could have made Ted Williams a second Babe Ruth, for he might have become not only the greatest, but the most popular big-league player since the Babe. Instead, Williams's entire career was blighted by intense personality problems, and these problems actually changed the face of baseball.

The question, "What's the matter with the Red Sox?" was first asked during Ted's rookie year, 1939. It would then be repeated annually—when they finished fourth behind Detroit, Cleveland, and New York in 1940 and second behind the Yankees in 1941 and 1942—right up to World War II and again after the 1946 pennant.

Tom Yawkey was to make a few other moves that did not help the team. His appointment of Cronin as GM in the autumn of 1947 was a mistake, although it didn't seem so at the time. Cronin had been a great ballplayer and not a bad manager. He knew the players, was a good judge of talent (it was he who advised signing Dom DiMaggio when everyone else shied away because DiMaggio wore glasses and looked too small), and had a rich baseball background.

But Cronin was too much like Yawkey: he worshiped his players, was reluctant to fire incompetents, and was generous to a fault. Furthermore, Cronin and Yawkey were too close in age and friendship. By the time Cronin became GM, Yawkey, who was a few years older, had owned the club fourteen years. During that time he had absorbed a tremendous amount of baseball knowledge from a master,

Eddie Collins, whose advice he accepted and whose judgment he respected. If Yawkey decided at that point that
he knew enough about the game to take a more active part
in the decision-making, who could blame him?

But no one will ever know whether Yawkey took over
making those decisions because he felt it should be his role
or because Cronin proved inadequate as a general manager. Whatever the reason, there were key decisions to be
made after Collins was out of the Red Sox picture, and it's
possible that some of the wrong ones were made by
Yawkey.

It's also possible that Yawkey *didn't* make the decisions
—that he left them all up to Cronin. Either way, a number
of those decisions turned out to be very wrong indeed. If
they were Yawkey's, Cronin should have resigned. If they
were Cronin's, Yawkey let him keep the job too long.

I'm sure the answer lies somewhere in between. Yawkey
no doubt made some decisions without consulting Cronin,
though Cronin probably made very few without consulting Yawkey. In fact, the strength of the general manager's
office, which had been built up by Eddie Collins, was
badly sapped when Cronin took the job. And that could
be nobody's fault but Yawkey's.

CHAPTER 4

On the Mound

Luck plays a huge part in major-league baseball, as in all professional sports. It's all right to say that an athlete or a team makes its own breaks, takes advantage of the mistakes of opponents or, in a sense, forces its luck. But the fact remains that things are continually happening that are utterly uncontrollable. There is no way of avoiding serious injury if the circumstances are unavoidable, just as there is no way an experienced combat soldier can avoid a fatal bullet.

In the forty-odd years of Tom Yawkey's ownership, Red Sox pitchers have been loaded with luck, most of it bad. One of the first instances came well before World War II, when Lefty Grove, a Hall-of-Famer who lasted seventeen years in the big leagues, waited until Boston bought him before delivering up a sore arm. Grove was a magnificent pitcher of the old school and in the Walter Johnson tradition. His fast ball may have been the most baffling pitch ever thrown by a southpaw. He lived off it, and for years the teams he pitched for won pennants with it.

Grove's career in the majors didn't begin until he was in his mid-twenties, not because he wasn't ready but because the old International League Baltimore Orioles, who wanted big-league status, wouldn't let him go. The late Jack Dunn, who owned the team, built the best minor-league club in history around Grove, George Earnshaw, Joe Boley, Max Bishop, and others of similar caliber. For perhaps five years, Dunn tried to force his way into the majors by the sheer power of his ball club. There was never a doubt it could beat most existing big-league teams, no doubt at all that it qualified, in player personnel and city population, for major-league status. The only trouble was that at the time Dunn got this team of baseball giants together, the sixteen-club alignment that then existed in the two big leagues was a closed corporation, bounded on the north and east by Boston, on the south by Washington and on the west by St. Louis. Five cities, Boston, New York, Philadelphia, Chicago, and St. Louis, had teams in each league, constricting the majors even more. There was plenty of room for expansion, but the majors weren't ready for it, and wouldn't be for another quarter century or more.

By the time Dunn gave up—after his Orioles had won one International League pennant after another for years—his stars were already getting old. At that time, the mid-twenties, thirty was considered old for a ballplayer. And though it was not uncommon for a twenty-year-old to break into the majors, anyone over twenty-five was considered a bad risk, because he didn't figure to have many years left. Lefty Grove, the outstanding star of the Orioles, was a big-league pitcher long before he reached the Philadelphia Athletics, who bought him from Baltimore in 1925 after Dunn decided his quest for major-league recognition was hopeless. Grove, with not much more than his blazing fast ball, made his presence felt almost at once by leading both leagues in earned run percentages in 1926. Later he would pile up some amazing records, mostly with the Athletics.

He was the major league ERA leader four times, all with the A's. He led the American League nine times, five with the A's, four with the Red Sox. He won fourteen straight games for the A's in 1928 and sixteen straight for them in 1931. He still leads all American League southpaw pitchers in strikeouts with 2266. He won twenty or more games seven years in succession (including a thirty-one-game season in 1931) at Philadelphia, then won twenty again for Boston in 1935.

Besides proving Grove's greatness as a pitcher, these statistics also bear out how much more effective he was in Philadelphia than in Boston. He was among the first of many great stars Yawkey purchased from Connie Mack's Athletics. When he went to Boston he had never had a sore arm, beyond the early twinges almost all pitchers suffer when they begin spring training. But his arm bothered him right into the regular season of his first year with the Red Sox, and it became a full-blown sore arm in 1936.

So the Lefty Grove Boston paid six figures for was the real Lefty Grove for only a season or two at Fenway. He then had to become a new pitcher so he could continue to win in the American League. He succeeded in this effort, but the Lefty Grove who starred for the Red Sox through the 1938 season was not a fast ball pitcher at all, but a crafty big-league veteran who got by on a good curve, great control, and a thorough knowledge of the opposition.

When he won the three-hundredth and last game of his major-league career in 1941 he was past forty and a bare shell of his former self. That three-hundredth victory came hard, and only by courtesy of Joe Cronin and Tom Yawkey. Both knew Grove was through, but they wanted him to win three hundred as badly as Grove did. Cronin kept him in the regular pitching rotation for weeks, but the old star was repeatedly belted out of the box before the fifth inning, the minimum he had to pitch in order to get credit for a victory. At long last, he struggled through six innings before leaving for the showers, and his teammates managed to hold the lead for him, giving him that three-hundredth win. He never won another game and at the end of the season, Lefty Grove retired.

Grove's was the first of many sore arms suffered by Red Sox pitchers. Other teams saw sore-armed stars suddenly go down the drain, but none as many as the Red Sox. The sore-arm pitching jinx was the worst of several bad breaks that Boston has suffered during Yawkey's ownership. No question that this was an unlucky ball club as, indeed, it is to this day. And most of the bad luck befell pitchers, which is why the Red Sox have never been free of trouble on the mound except in 1946.

Perhaps the most glaring case was 1947. When the ballplayers reported for spring training at Sarasota, they had their four stars from 1946—Boo Ferriss, Tex Hughson, Mickey Harris, and Joe Dobson—plus several rookies who looked as if they couldn't possibly miss. Joe Cronin, in his last year as manager, thought sure the club would repeat on pitching alone. So did just about everyone else.

Four rookies looked particularly good in spring training. Mel Parnell, who later became a standout, still holds most Red Sox records for southpaws. But in 1947 he wasn't ready, and when he went to the minors he suffered a badly broken finger on his pitching hand. Parnell would go on to some outstanding seasons, but 1947 wouldn't be one of them.

A lanky youngster named Al Widmar looked like another sure winner, but he went to the minors and never amounted to anything. Tommy Fine also seemed to have a marvelous career in front of him, but it was so far ahead that he never caught up with it. The fourth promising rookie at spring training in 1947 was Harry Dorish, a chunky youth from the Pennsylvania coal-mining region. Eventually, he became a good relief pitcher, but he never made it big.

So after two weeks at Sarasota, the 1946 powerhouse ball club had no less than eight pitchers who might well have been of starting caliber in 1947. Of the four rookies, only Dorish stayed all season. As for the men who had pitched the team to the 1946 pennant, what happened to three of them—and to the Red Sox—shouldn't have happened to a dog.

Ferriss, Hughson, and Harris came up with sore arms. Since almost all pitchers have sore arms at the start of spring training, nobody thought much about it at first. During Joe Cronin's daily press conferences at the Sarasota Terrace Hotel, he continually assured us there was nothing to worry about. I'm sure he really felt that way for a while, but when the weeks went by without any improvement in those three priceless arms, even this eternal optimist began to have doubts.

By the time the team came north for the opening of the season, the situation had become serious. Joe Dobson was the only one who could pitch with his usual form. The other three were still plagued with the miseries, as they would be for the rest of their careers.

Tex Hughson had only himself to blame. A tall right-hander with more brains than the average professional athlete, he actually outsmarted himself. Hughson was one of the few men left on the club who had been a teammate of Lefty Grove's in 1941. He had seen Grove's frustrating struggle for his three-hundredth win, and it had made a deep impression on him. The following year, Hughson won twenty-two games, then spent the next three in the service, but he still couldn't get Grove's experience out of his mind.

A student of pitching, Hughson had plenty of time to think about the fate of good pitchers when they get too old to win in the big leagues. During his service years, he tried to look ahead into the future to see what was in store for him. The result of all this thinking was a schedule that sounded logical, not only to Hughson but to everyone else with whom he discussed it. During the 1946 season, while he was winning twenty games, he often explained the pattern of pitching he had laid out for himself.

"I saw what happened to Grove," he said. "The guy depended on his great fast ball for years, but everyone knows you can't live on that forever. When he hurt his arm he had to start all over again—sharpen his curve, develop his changeup, work on his control, build a repertoire of off-speed pitches. He had a few good years with the Red Sox, but he should have had more.

"Now the big trouble with Grove," Hughson went on, "was that he made the same mistake all fast ball pitchers make. Instead of looking ahead to when he would lose it, he thought it would last forever. He should have learned those other pitches when he was younger. And that's what I'm going to do. By the time I lose my fast ball I'll have three or four other effective pitches. They'll help me now and prolong my career later."

Tex Hughson was not the kind of man to make many a mistake, but when he did, it was a beaut. While he was still blinding the opposition with one of the best fast balls in the league, he began working on other pitches—curves, sinkers, changes, knucklers (the slider wasn't a standard pitch yet and very few pitchers used it at the time). Hughson's thinking made sense except for one thing; he left out Mother Nature. A baseball pitcher with an outstanding fast ball can rely on it only by throwing it constantly, and he can do that only when he is young and strong. If it's good enough, he doesn't need anything else. A man with Hughson's speed could challenge hitters with fast balls all day. Except for an occasional changeup thrown with the same motion, he shouldn't monkey seriously with any other kind of pitch. If he does, he'll surely jeopardize the one pitch that got him into the majors and kept him there. Few batters will hit a fast ball safely, not only because they can't get a good look at it but because a really good fast one will hop, sink, or move around in some other way. Most important, it is thrown with a natural motion, without twisting wrist or elbow, which cuts down the chance of a sore arm.

By working on other pitches—the ones he felt he'd need later—all Hughson succeeded in doing was to ruin his fast ball. He experimented himself right out of business and the Red Sox right out of a pennant chance. Too late, he discovered his mistake. When he tried to rectify it he had lost the fast ball that had been his money pitch. And Tex Hughson without a fast ball was like a cone without ice cream—an empty shell with no substance. Hughson spent several more years with the Red Sox and pitched a few good games, but he was never again a star. In 1947 he won twelve games and lost eleven.

Nobody, least of all the man himself, knows what happened to Mickey Harris. Younger than Hughson and apparently with almost as good a future ahead of him, Harris in 1947 just couldn't throw the way he had in 1946. I had my own thoughts about why this was so, and when I mentioned my conjecture to him, he agreed it might be a possibility.

Harris, a left-hander, had just bought a new house in the Boston suburb of Winchester. When I went to interview him for an off-season story one winter's day, he was paneling his basement walls to serve as a playroom for his children and a bar for parties. It didn't occur to me at the time, but when his sore arm developed, I remembered seeing him on a ladder, reaching up with his left arm to put in the paneling. Doing that all winter could tire anyone's arm. And, it seemed to me, could also wreck the arm of a baseball pitcher. Anyhow, Harris ended up with the worst record of the three Red Sox pitching cripples of 1947. He won five games and lost four, and never again had a good season.

The third sore-armed pitcher was Boo Ferriss. Nobody could figure his difficulty either. He had been a twenty-five-game winner in 1946 and a twenty-one-game winner in 1945, but his 1947 record was the same as Hughson's—twelve wins and eleven losses. The two 1946 aces couldn't win as many games between them the next year as Ferriss had won alone.

Much later, Joe Dobson told me that when it finally was obvious that Ferriss's arm would never come back, everyone on the team who had heard about his background begged him to try to pitch left-handed.

"All those stories about how well he could throw lefty weren't completely malarkey," Dobson said. "I saw him do it and he wasn't bad. I don't know whether he could have been a successful big-league southpaw, but he certainly had a lot of stuff. I sure would have liked to see him try."

"Why didn't he?" I asked.

Dobson shrugged.

"Who knows?" he said. "Pride maybe. Lack of confidence in his left arm. A feeling that his right arm would come back. Ferriss was a big, powerful man. There's no doubt he could *throw* lefty. Whether he could *pitch* lefty was something else again. After all, Fenway Park is not exactly a paradise for left-handers with that close left field wall. Few lefties did well there because they usually had to face lineups packed with right-handed batters. Still, Boo might have fooled everyone if he'd tried. He sure as hell had lost his effectiveness as a right-hander. What could he lose trying to switch?"

It was an interesting possibility, remote though it sounded. To my knowledge, there has never been a big-league player who could successfully throw ambidextrously, though there are plenty of switch hitters. If Ferriss had tried to pitch left-handed in 1947 and had

succeeded in winning, he would have become the only
major-league pitcher in history to do so. Instead, like
Hughson and Harris, he sat on the Red Sox bench for several years and finally threw in the towel. Later, he came
back as a pitching coach under Mike Higgins, then drifted
out of professional baseball into college coaching.

Despite the calamitous loss of three of their four front-
line pitchers, the 1947 Red Sox, picked virtually unanimously to win the pennant, didn't do badly. The slack was
taken up by a collection of fairly good pitchers, but not
one who had the quality of the 1946 big four.

Denny Galehouse, bought from Cleveland to beef up
the pitching staff (the Red Sox were—and still are—always
buying or trading for ballplayers to "beef up" the club
somewhere), won eleven games. Earl Johnson won thirteen, many in relief. Dorish won seven and lost eight, not
bad for a rookie. Eventually, he found his strength as a
relief pitcher—but for the White Sox, not the Red Sox.

The man who saved the club from utter chaos was Dobson, who had a better year in 1947 than in 1946. He won
eighteen and lost eight while compiling a 2.95 ERA, and
was the ace of the pitching staff. If he'd done better
against New York, Boston might still have finished the season in second place, instead of third. But Dobson lost five
games to the Yankees without beating them all year. And
they breezed to the pennant fourteen games ahead of the
Red Sox and twelve ahead of the Tigers. Dobson wasn't
the only man on the staff to have trouble with the Bomb-
ers, however. Of twenty-two games against New York,
Boston won only eight.

The hitters certainly did their best. Ted Williams won

his second Triple Crown, with a .343 batting average, 32 homers, and 114 runs batted in. He also led the league in runs, total bases, walks, and slugging percentage.

Two other Red Sox players had more than 200 hits and batted over .300. One was Johnny Pesky, his third year in the big leagues and his third with over 200 hits. He batted .324. The other was a rookie right fielder, Sam Mele, who batted .302 with 203 hits. As a team, the Red Sox batted .265. They also drew a record attendance for that time of 1,427,315, breaking the mark they had set in their pennant-winning season of 1946. They played their first night game in 1947 to a jammed house of nearly 35,000 people, including 2000 standees.

Because of all the sore pitching arms, Boston failed to dominate the opposition at home, as they had in 1946. Instead of winning sixty-one games in Fenway Park, they won forty-nine while losing thirty. And on the road, where they had won nine more games than they lost the year before, they won only thirty-four games while losing forty-one. Teams rarely win pennants with losing records on the road, no matter what they do at home.

Had 1947 been the only season that Tom Yawkey's Red Sox were plagued by bad luck, this would not have been an important factor in the club's everlasting failure to win pennants that should have been theirs. But the three sore-armed pitching stars of 1947—to say nothing of Lefty Grove and a few lesser lights before them—weren't the only baffling cases. Because this ball club has always had mysterious troubles with pitchers, and they continue to today.

There was Maurice McDermott, tabbed the "typical

baseball rookie" in 1948. A long, skinny Irishman from
New Jersey with an engaging grin, the freshness of youth
(he was only nineteen), and a blazing fast ball, McDermott reminded everyone of Grove. Of all the kid pitchers
I have ever seen in spring training, he was the most impressive. A left-hander who had thrown two no-hitters in
the Eastern League the year before, he laughed his way
through the Red Sox training camp and seemed certain to
be a smashing combination of all the extraordinary southpaws in major-league history. He was wild, just as most
rookie left-handers are wild, but with his speed it seemed
certain that the stars in his twinkling blue eyes were indi-
cations of things to come. When he pitched batting practice, veteran hitters stood at the plate wondering whether
to swing or duck. If McDermott could just learn to get the
ball over the plate consistently, greatness would be his.

Instead, McDermott became a classic Red Sox pitching
failure. Hopelessly inconsistent, he would turn in about
one good game in five. The other four were nightmares of
wildness which kept him from ever achieving his promise.
For a while he accepted his fate with the same big grin
that had captivated everyone at spring training. A tenor
of minor talent, who occasionally sang in night clubs
around Boston during the off-season, he used to convulse
teammates by cupping his hands around a baseball, cock-
ing his head, and crooning, "Li'l ball, why won't you go
over the plate for me?"

When it did go over the plate, everything looked rosy.
McDermott once pitched a near-perfect game at Fenway
Park, an amazing achievement for a left-hander. The lead-
off batter in the first inning hit a bleeding single that just

trickled through the infield, then was erased on a double play. McDermott retired the next twenty-five men in a row for a one-hitter in which he faced the minimum twenty-seven batters.

But more often he was yanked after walking three or four men in a row. Together with two other Boston pitchers and two or three from Cleveland, he once participated in a record eighteen-walk game, a battle of passes lasting nearly four hours. But McDermott always looked so promising that the Red Sox held onto him for six years before giving up. And although several other clubs were to try him, he never could harness his fast ball and finally faded into oblivion.

At this writing the jury is still out on Ken Brett, another hot rookie southpaw. He looked so good in the minors that the Sox put him on their eligible list for the 1967 World Series less than a month after he turned nineteen. He appeared in two games against the Cardinals, holding them hitless for a total of one and a third innings, while fans oohed and ahed at his blinding fast ball.

So what happened? The following season Ken Brett came up with a sore arm at Louisville, and he's been struggling ever since. Boston finally gave up on him the winter following the 1971 season and traded him to Milwaukee, where, by the summer of 1972 he was doing fairly well. The following winter the Brewers traded him to Philadelphia.

Twin frustrations of major proportions were a couple of buddies named Jerry Stephenson and Dave Morehead. Both had ability coming out of their ears, but, with the exception of a Morehead no-hitter in 1965, that was the only place it showed. Morehead finally ended his career

after several unhappy seasons with the inevitable sore
arm. Stephenson, whose father, Joe, was and still is a Red
Sox west-coast scout, didn't seem to want to be successful.
He once jumped the club to drive back and forth across
the country for a while before rejoining the team. Occasionally he'd even pitch a good game, and all sorts of
wonderful things would again be predicted for him. But
the only thing he ever contributed was his signature on a
considerable bonus check for signing. Like Brett, Morehead and Stephenson were both eligible for the 1967
World Series, but for all the good they did they might as
well have stood in bed.

Dick Radatz, a huge fast ball pitcher, had two good
years as a relief artist—he won sixteen games in relief in
1964—before going the way of most promising Boston
hurlers. Big as he was, he burned himself out and was
through long before the team's Impossible Dream season. I
don't know whether or not it means anything in terms of
Red Sox bad luck, but Radatz's roommate at Michigan
State, Ron Perranoski, was a successful relief pitcher for
over ten years with the Dodgers, the Twins, and the Tigers.
It makes me wonder if Radatz would have lasted longer
with a different ball club.

Two other Red Sox rookies who started their careers like
lions and ended like lambs were Tom Brewer and Don
Schwall. Brewer won nineteen games before collapsing on
a heap of unfulfilled promises. Schwall was well on his way
toward winning twenty games as a rookie in 1960 when he
was felled by a kidney ailment in midseason, after which
he never regained his effectiveness.

Earl Wilson and Bill Monbouquette pitched no-hitters

for the Red Sox in 1962, and the following year Monbouquette was a twenty-game winner. Although both showed occasional flashes of form, neither did anything more than mildly sensational again; and the Red Sox finally traded them. Although Monbouquette continued to have trouble, Wilson became a twenty-game winner for Detroit, which he had never been in Boston.

This was a typical Red Sox problem. Bad luck dogged them even after they let hopefuls go elsewhere. Once out of Boston uniforms, too many players performed well for somebody else. Wilson, although disappointing at Fenway, was a pretty solid pitcher, as he proved when he joined the Tigers.

There was also the strange case of Frank Baumann. A chubby right-hander with a fast ball, Baumann attracted practically every club in the majors. He had money-waving scouts on his St. Louis doorstep the day he graduated from high school. The Red Sox outbid everyone else, giving Baumann something over $100,000 to sign. If ever a boy looked like the whiz kid to end all whiz kids, it was Baumann. At Louisville, Boston's Triple A farm, he had a strong season. He then went into the service—and came out with a sore arm.

It was the same old story with a slightly different twist. The Red Sox stuck with Baumann a few years, even though he spent most of his time in the bullpen. What happened next was no tribute to the Boston pitching coach at the time, which may be one reason for their constant problems.

At Fenway Park, the home and visiting bullpens are joined end to end, separated by a wire screen. Once, after several years of going nowhere, Baumann was warming up in the bullpen during a game against Chicago. Ray Berres, the White Sox bullpen coach, a former catcher and a keen observer of pitchers, watched Baumann idly at first, then began studying him. Later Berres went to Manager Al Lopez and said, "If you get Baumann, I think I can help him."

So when Chicago made an offer for the one-time school-boy hot shot, the Red Sox, who had given up on him any-how, happily dealt him off. Berres helped him correct a technical problem which any good pitching coach should have spotted, and Baumann became a successful relief hurler, lasting with the White Sox for several years.

The Red Sox even walked into one sore-armed pitching situation with their eyes wide open, because a new man-ager insisted on getting rid of Dick Stuart. Billy Herman, who had had plenty of time to observe Stuart while coach-ing under Johnny Pesky, succeeded Pesky as manager near the end of the 1964 season. The first thing Herman did was order Stuart out of the Fenway Park scene.

He had good reason to do so. Stuart was a wise-cracking first baseman whose worst problem was such a marked in-ability to field that he willingly answered to the name "Dr. Strangeglove." He spent half the time counting his home runs and the other half waving at easy grounders going by. An aggravating braggart in the locker room, he didn't care if the team won or lost as long as he drove one out of the park, which he did 228 times during his career.

The Red Sox had so much trouble peddling Stuart that they had to settle for an even swap with the Phillies, who were willing to give up Dennis Bennett, a southpaw pitcher with a history of arm trouble. The Phillies, however, assured Boston that Bennett was all right, and when the trade was made, everyone thought he was.

They were wrong. When Bennett showed up at spring training camp in 1965 with a sore arm, the Phillies offered to nullify the deal. But since that would mean taking Stuart back, the Red Sox decided to keep Bennett. The only ones who benefited from that decision were the members of the press, who used up miles of copy in the next two years discussing Bennett's arm and his chances of ever becoming an effective pitcher. A hopeless case from the start, Bennett finally faded back into obscurity.

But the most obvious bit of unnecessary bad luck was the Jim Lonborg case. A Stanford graduate with a supposed modicum of common sense, Lonborg showed none at all the winter following his marvelous 1967 season. His twenty-two victories paced the Red Sox to the pennant and won Lonborg the Cy Young award as baseball's best pitcher that year. Not only was he a twin hero with Carl Yastrzemski, but at twenty-five he seemed to be a Boston fixture for years to come.

Until Lonborg discovered skiing that winter. Despite warnings from the ball club and even from a few Boston sports columnists (including Tim Horgan of the *Herald Traveler* and me), Lonborg didn't see how a trained athlete could possibly suffer a crippling injury in such a universally popular sport.

He found out how one disastrous December day when, skiing down a California slope near Lake Tahoe, he lost his footing and wrenched his knee. Even a clean leg break would have been better. That, at least, would have healed quickly, and he might have been ready to pitch by opening day. Instead, he smashed some ligaments, leaving not only his career, but all hopes the Red Sox had of repeating their 1967 pennant, on that hill in California.

His forgiving fans thought nothing was quite as touching as Lonborg's game battle to come back. But as far as the Red Sox were concerned, it was all in vain. He had done his teammates a gross injustice by skiing at all, and the six victories he finally won in 1968 were only a token help in the club's fourth-place finish.

To further aggravate their pitching troubles, Jose Santiago, the team's second best pitcher in 1967, reported to spring training with about the millionth sore arm in the history of Yawkey's ownership of the club. Although they had traded for two seasoned National League pitchers, Ray Culp and Dick Ellsworth, after Lonborg's skiing injury, there was no way the Red Sox could go anywhere in 1968.

From the beginning of that season to the end, Manager Dick Williams never mentioned Lonborg's folly. And even a few years later, after he had managed the Oakland A's to the American League West Division title in 1971, the subject was still a touchy one with Williams. Simply too gruesome to talk about.

At this writing, Lonborg, who went to Milwaukee after the 1971 season in the same deal with Brett and to Philadelphia with Brett after the 1972 season, is doing fairly well. Perhaps he has finally come all the way back. If so, the bad luck he wished on his team when he took up skiing may be compounded. If he becomes a winner he won't be the first Red Sox pitcher to find resurrection in another club's uniform.

One of the strangest cases of bad pitching luck was that of Ray Scarborough. This marvelously amiable character held a hex over the Red Sox for years when he pitched for Washington. In desperation, Boston finally got him in a trade, only to discover that while he could beat them, he couldn't win for them. So at last they dealt him off to the Yankees. One of his first starts in New York was against his old team. He threw a two-hit shutout at them.

There's no accounting for luck.

Which is why, when somebody asks, "What's the matter with the Red Sox?" one of the answers has to be, "They're unlucky." When it comes to pitchers, nobody could be unluckier.

CHAPTER 5

In the Dugout

The Red Sox don't make a practice of hiring mediocre managers, but even their better ones seem to develop mediocrity when they don the uniform. The best
manager since Yawkey bought the club has been Dick Williams. He was fired after the 1969 season for several reasons, although the one promoted by the management was
that he had lost communication with his players. This was
partially true, for Williams exhibited one serious weakness
in Boston. When one of his ballplayers failed to perform
up to snuff, Williams would treat him like a pariah for
anywhere from a week to a season. He got so mad at
George Scott—who might yet become an outstanding star
if he will follow advice—that he wouldn't speak to Scott
two years after he left the Red Sox.

But when Williams was fired, even close observers of the
ball club were surprised. Aside from the fact that he had
another year to go on his contract, he had continued to do
a good job and to take no nonsense from his ballplayers.

In actual point of fact, Williams was fired by Tom

Yawkey personally because Williams objected to a newspaper story by Clif Keane of the Boston *Globe*. Early in the season Keane asked Yawkey to rate Williams as a manager on a scale of one to four, with one the highest. Yawkey rated Williams three, next to the lowest on the scale.

When Williams read the story, he went right to Yawkey and asked, "Is this how you really feel about me or did Keane misquote you?"

"I wasn't misquoted," the Red Sox owner replied.

"Mr. Yawkey," Williams said, "I don't care about myself, but this doesn't help the ball club one bit. I don't think your coming into the locker room as often as you do helps either. Too many times I've eaten someone out for a mistake and then seen you put your arm around his shoulder as if to comfort him."

The whole conversation was low-key—almost friendly— but when it ended there was no question that Williams's days in Boston were numbered. He wasn't actually fired until shortly before the season was over. Notified on the day of a night game at Fenway, he told two of his coaches, then managed the team to a win that evening. Bobby Doerr, the batting coach and former Red Sox star, was so upset by the incident that he resigned when the season ended.

With another year to go on a three-year contract, Williams could have collected his full salary sitting out the 1970 season. Instead, he became a Montreal coach under Manager Gene Mauch, with the Red Sox paying him the difference between his new salary and the larger amount he would have been paid in Boston. And what Williams

learned from Mauch undoubtedly stood him in good stead
for the future.

As the whole baseball world knows, the next year Williams became manager of the Oakland A's. He led them to
the American League West Division title in 1971, his first
year, and then to the world championship in 1972. He now
ranks among the most successful managers in baseball.

Even before Dick Williams verified the facts leading to
his dismissal, it wasn't hard to determine that he had been
fired by Yawkey, who personally had given him the three-
year contract in a well-publicized conference after the Impossible Dream victory of 1967. And it was also apparent
that neither Dick O'Connell, the general manager, nor
Haywood Sullivan, the player personnel director, was in
favor of the move, though neither would admit it. O'Connell had hired Williams for the 1967 season on Sullivan's
recommendation, and it wasn't easy for them to hide the
fact that they were upset when he left. So were a lot of
other people around Boston.

That firing was a rare example of reverse cronyism on
Yawkey's part. During his forty years of ownership he has
rarely either personally fired or demanded the elimination
of someone in his employ. The only others I am aware of
were Birdie Tebbetts and Jimmy Piersall.

Williams's real trouble in Boston wasn't so much his extreme toughness as the fact that he was becoming a regrettably nice guy. The man who practically horsewhipped
the Red Sox to the pennant in 1967 grew softer and softer
in the next two years. The quality which had given him
strength and had enabled him to control the ball club was
his severity. Without that, he was just another manager.

And if he had stayed in Boston much longer, he might have become exactly that.

Although by 1969 he was perceptibly easing up on his ballplayers, Williams was the only Yawkey manager since Cronin to really have the courage of his convictions. Like his predecessors, Williams started out by threatening suitable punishment to men who loafed, played harder off the field than on, worried more about their personal records than the ball club's, and considered their outside interests more important than baseball.

The players had always tested Williams's predecessors first with small infractions, then had become bolder and bolder until by midseason they were doing as they pleased while the manager stood by helplessly and let them get away with everything short of murder.

When Williams made the same threats other managers had, a close Red Sox observer shrugged his shoulders and said, "Hold your hats, girls, here we go again." One sports commentator, after interviewing Williams on the subject of discipline before the beginning of the 1967 season, played tapes of similar interviews with his three predecessors: Billy Herman, Johnny Pesky, and Mike Higgins. They all sounded the same.

The others tried, but they never backed up their threats with action. Williams did. After he had levied a few fines and made them stick, his noble athletes fell into line, then went about the business of winning the pennant. Few actually liked Williams, although he was a warm, friendly man off the field, but they played ball for him.

He worked them harder in spring training than any previous Red Sox manager had. At the training base in Winter

Haven, Florida, he made the bachelors and men who had
left their families home stay at the headquarters hotel
where he could keep an eye on them. He announced that
no sore-armed pitchers would go to Boston when the club
broke camp, and instituted a rigorous training schedule that
allowed no time for loafing. Instead of gripes and whines,
the players reacted with an enthusiasm and team spirit
that no Boston team had shown for years.

The keynote of the 1967 season was sounded by Dennis
Bennett when the Red Sox, at Williams's insistence, let him
go early in the year. The day he left, Bennett said, "It's a
hell of a ball club and Williams is a hell of a manager." He
was right on both counts. Nobody had referred to any
other modern Red Sox field boss as "a hell of a manager."
The reason was that, although some managers occasionally
showed a few small signs of genius, their inconsistencies
were far more conspicuous.

Joe Cronin was probably as good a field leader as he was
allowed to be. But when he became general manager after
the 1947 season, his own managerial appointments were
poor. The first, in 1948, was Joe McCarthy, who was little
more than the reflection of a romance Cronin had been
carrying on for years with New York. Partial to the ball
clubs, the players, the managers, even the press in New
York, Cronin often spoke as if Boston were a cow town by
comparison.

Cronin's partiality to New York probably cost Boston
the 1948 and 1949 pennants. Although the decision to hire
McCarthy was made a year in advance, as Yawkey had confided to some Boston baseball writers just before the Red
Sox clinched the 1946 pennant, it is almost certain that

Cronin selected him. Cronin had always admired Mc-
Carthy and openly raved about him when the Yankees
were winning pennants. McCarthy did lead New York to
eight pennants and seven world championships; but any
good baseball man should have won with the clubs they
had in the thirties and forties, spearheaded by Joe DiMaggio. All the way through 1964, when they won their last
pennant, the Yankees made one manager after another
look great.

By the end of the 1946 season, McCarthy was available,
since the Yankees had fired him the previous May. Cronin's
first public move after becoming general manager was to
announce with obvious satisfaction that McCarthy "was
coming out of retirement to manage the Red Sox." Then,
with the help of a huge chunk of Yawkey's money and
two deals with the impoverished St. Louis Browns, Cronin
presented McCarthy with a ball club, complete with pitchers, that should have won for any self-respecting manager.
Even considering the holdover sore arms from 1947, the
Red Sox teams of 1948 and 1949 were two of history's best.
Many Boston observers thought McCarthy did a magnificent job by bringing those clubs to the last day before losing. Actually, neither pennant race should have been that
close.

After the 1947 disaster, the Red Sox had made two mammoth deals with the Browns which should have insured
pennants no matter what. Although these trades were announced separately, they were probably made at the same
time. And the men Boston acquired not only filled a crying
need for right-handed starting pitchers—only Joe Dobson
was still sound—but gave them a hammering right-handed

slugger, as well as one of the best utility men in the business.

First the Red Sox disclosed that they had sent three substitutes and $65,000 in cash to St. Louis for right-hander Ellis Kinder and infielder Billy Hitchcock. But the real whopper was withheld until the next day when Boston gave the Browns seven more players of mediocre or unproved ability and $310,000 for right-hander Jack Kramer and slugging shortstop Vernon (Junior) Stephens.

So for about half a million dollars in cash and some expendable players, they all but nailed the 1948 pennant to the mast. The only question was whether to keep Pesky at short and move Stephens to third or do it the other way around. The club that went south in 1948 appeared to have little room for any rookies other than pitchers. Jake Jones was on first, Bobby Doerr at second, Stephens and Pesky at short and third, with Ted Williams, Dom DiMaggio, and Sam Mele in the outfield. The catcher was Birdie Tebbetts, obtained in a 1947 trade with Detroit. Starting right-handed pitchers were Dobson, Kramer, and Kinder. For southpaws there were two hot rookies, Mel Parnell and Maurice McDermott, while the bullpen was loaded with good relievers. Except for Jones and Mele this was the club that played most of the season.

Billy Goodman, a rookie line drive hitter who could play almost anywhere, succeeded Jones when it became apparent that Jones couldn't do anything at the plate but pop the ball up. For reasons best known to himself, McCarthy took an instant dislike to Mele, whom he benched despite Mele's great rookie season the previous year. McCarthy then informed the front office that he needed a right fielder and was duly presented with Al Zarilla and Stan Spence, who split the job between them. McCarthy also decided to leave Stephens at short and put Pesky on third.

This ball club, with all its new and expensive talent, would have been odds-on favorites to win the pennant in 1948 no matter who the manager was. But with McCarthy, that New York living legend, at the helm, the Red Sox seemed to have everything wrapped up before the season began.

McCarthy may have been a living legend in New York, but in Boston he was a dying swan. The man who figured to leave town trailing a string of pennants is today remembered only as the manager who, with three strong young pitchers ready, threw Denny Galehouse, a has-been in his mid-thirties, against the Cleveland Indians in a one-game playoff for the 1948 American League pennant. As expected, Galehouse got his brains beaten out, and the team that couldn't miss blew everything.

It may seem surprising that a man who was such a giant in New York should leave as his only Boston managerial monument an absurd pitching selection in the most important game of the season, but it must be admitted that McCarthy asked for it. So did the Red Sox, when they hired him in the first place. There was no more reason for them to offer McCarthy the job than for McCarthy to take it. From the Red Sox standpoint there were plenty of good men available. And from McCarthy's, there was nothing to gain. He had all the money he needed, he could look back on a sensational series of triumphs, and he would have been much happier leading the life of a gentleman farmer in upstate New York, as at this writing he is doing.

He went to Boston with no more worlds to conquer. He
had led the Cubs to the 1929 National League pennant before moving to the Yankees two years later. He had won
his first Yankee pennant in 1932. He was the only man to
manage both Babe Ruth and Joe DiMaggio. Seven of his
Yankee players—Ruth, DiMaggio, Lou Gehrig, Lefty Go-
mez, Bill Dickey, Herb Pennock, and Red Ruffing—are now
in baseball's Hall of Fame. McCarthy's reputation was so
secure that he himself is one of only four Hall of Fame
managers.

There were also some less obvious reasons why Mc-
Carthy and the Red Sox should never have been brought
together. McCarthy loved Broadway, the adulation of the
biggest show city in the world, the spotlight that always
shone on him while he managed the Yankees, a celebrity
among celebrities.

McCarthy came to Boston with just enough disdain so
it showed. He talked of his great New York teams with
pride, making it clear that the Red Sox could never take
the place of the Yankees in his heart. He spoke of his show-
business friends, always pointing out that while they'd
passed through Boston, they had gone on to New York to
stay. McCarthy didn't think he belonged in Boston; compared to New York, it just wasn't big league. He didn't
think the Red Sox could carry the bats of his beloved
Yankees, and it showed all over.

But to the Red Sox people, he was a baseball immortal
to be admired, looked up to: the man to lead the Red Sox
out of the wilderness of second place. Ask any of the Boston brass from that time about McCarthy, and you will get
the same answers today you got then—he was the greatest,

absolutely the greatest. And you'll get the same answers from most of the ballplayers who worked for him in Boston —Williams, Bobby Doerr, Johnny Pesky, Dom DiMaggio, Mel Parnell, Jack Kramer, Birdie Tebbetts. They all apparently thought he really was great, and those still alive today remember him as great.

Yet none of them could tell me *why* he was great. I got the same answer from everyone I asked, meaningless to me then and still meaningless to me today.

"He left you alone . . ."

If that is the mark of a great manager, why did the Red Sox fire Dick Williams, who, they said, had lost communication with his ballplayers? McCarthy never *had* any communication with his. He spent most of the time before games in his office, usually alone or with one of his coaches. He neither sought nor accepted advice. When he called ballplayers in, which he did occasionally, they went with sinking heart and measured tread because they were scared to death of him. He was the school principal, they the kids caught throwing spitballs.

His reputation for handling players was based on one or two incidents involving superstars, of whom he had had several in New York. In Boston, he had Ted Williams. His best-known, and perhaps only, contact with Williams was a remote-control gesture which McCarthy knew would make a big impression on everybody. Ted Williams refused to wear a necktie. As manager of the Yankees, McCarthy had insisted that his ballplayers look like gentlemen out of uniform, and that meant wearing neckties. But he knew Williams wouldn't. So, on his first morning as active manager, McCarthy appeared at breakfast in the coffee shop of the Sarasota Terrace Hotel without a necktie and with his shirt open at the collar. From that day on, Williams thought he was the greatest manager who ever lived. So did others who saw the incident.

McCarthy did nothing else to distinguish himself as a manager in Boston. Certainly, he didn't try to manage Williams, but when McCarthy appeared on the Boston scene, how much managing did Williams need? He knew more about hitting than any man alive or dead. His immortality as a ballplayer was assured, if for no other reason than that he was the last of the .400 hitters. (.406 in 1941.) As McCarthy himself said when asked about Williams, "The manager who can't get along with a .400 hitter ought to have his head examined."

Even with the last of the .400 hitters, a lineup and batting order that looked like an all-star team, a good pitching rotation, "the best manager in baseball," and tremendous crowds every day, the Red Sox got off to a dismal start. By Memorial Day they were in seventh place, eleven and a half games off the pace and barely ahead of the cellar-dwelling White Sox.

Rarely has the cry, "What's the matter with the Red Sox?" been louder, more anguished, or more impossible to answer. The last man to ask it of was Joe McCarthy, who blew his stack every time the subject arose. His stock answer to questions was, "You take care of your business and I'll take care of mine." He talked about everything except his current ball club—Babe Ruth, Lou Gehrig, Joe DiMaggio, Broadway, New York's celebrities. In fact, the only way to get him talking was to put him on his favorite subject, New York. But at the slightest reference to the

1948 Red Sox, he would clam up, and red splotches of anger would appear on his face.

Only once did McCarthy refer without impatience to the club that threatened to become baseball's flop of the century. About a week before Memorial Day, an out-of-town writer (the prying Boston scribes couldn't get anything out of him by then) asked what Marse Joe intended to do to put the club on a winning track.

"Nothing," he replied.

"Nothing?" the writer repeated.

"That's right," McCarthy said. "A great ball club will find its own level. This is a great ball club. And its own level is the top, not seventh place."

Although only a crumb, that statement was perhaps the key to McCarthy's astounding past success. He knew great ball clubs, because they were the only kind he had ever managed in the big leagues. He had won with them by letting them find their own level. In retrospect, I began to understand a little of what his players meant when they said, "He left you alone."

McCarthy left the team alone and because they *were* fundamentally a great ball club, they began climbing out of the hole they had dug for themselves. By the first weekend of August they were fourth, trailing Cleveland, New York, and Philadelphia in that order. The clubs were so closely bunched, however, that on August 23 Boston was able to move into the lead, where they stayed for five weeks.

By then, since the Athletics had dropped behind, it was a three-way race among the Red Sox, the Indians, and the Yankees. The clubs rocked back and forth right up to the last few days of the season. Near the end, with all three still in the running, I asked McCarthy what he thought.

He glared at me for a long moment, then shrugged his shoulders and said, "We do or we don't."

"We do or we don't." This was a reflection of McCarthy's whole philosophy: the result is in the hands of fate, and there's nothing anyone can do about it—I never forgot his words. They rose to the surface of my memory late in the 1967 season when the Red Sox were once again in the middle of a wild four-way pennant battle with the Twins, the Tigers, and the White Sox. When I asked Dick Williams the same question I had asked McCarthy at the same stage of the race nineteen years before, Williams snapped, "We'll win it." His answer was the difference between managing and nonmanaging.

Some people called McCarthy's attitude icy calm, but it really was a copout. The translation of "We do or we don't" is "It's the ballplayers who will win or lose it. What do you expect me to do?" The manager's role in a clutch spot is to radiate confidence and to transmit this to his men, to let them know he's sure they'll win and therefore *they* should be sure. Perhaps McCarthy didn't have to persuade his Yankee teams. They all radiated confidence anyhow.

But during the last week of 1948, the Red Sox went about the business of playing ball with the enthusiasm of clerks selling shoes. When you asked what they thought about the pennant race, most of them parroted their manager: "We do or we don't."

The only memorable thing McCarthy did was to make a rueful, somewhat sour prediction that came true. A few days before the end of the season, his Red Sox, Lou Boudreau's Indians, and Bucky Harris's Yankees were in a tie for top. "The guy who finishes third will lose his job," McCarthy said. He was right; the Yankees finished third, and Harris was replaced by Casey Stengel.

Boston fans, with the possibility of a subway World Series before them, since the Braves had already clinched the National League pennant, went crazy when the Red Sox eliminated the Yankees the day before the season ended. On the last day, a game behind the Indians, they again beat the Yankees, while the Indians lost to Detroit. That created a top tie between Boston and Cleveland and forced the one-game playoff for the pennant at Fenway Park on October 4.

Boudreau's pitcher was Gene Bearden, a rookie southpaw and twenty-game winner who had beaten the Tigers only two days before. Eager to pitch for the Red Sox were any one of the regular four starters—Kinder, Kramer, Dobson, or Parnell. Parnell, himself a rookie southpaw, had beaten the Yankees the day before, but insisted he was ready. His chances for the job were minimal, partly because he hadn't had enough rest, but mostly because the Indians were loaded with right-handed batters, and Fenway Park was usually no place for left-handers in clutch games. (Boudreau's selection of Bearden was not as surprising as it seemed, since his only other twenty-game winner was the left-handed Bob Lemon, who, like Parnell, had pitched the day before.)

Normally, McCarthy named his starting pitcher in plenty of time for him to take batting practice with the regulars and then loaf around the locker room until time for his pregame warmup. The rest of the pitchers would usually shag flies in the outfield.

But on this particular day McCarthy went into his office off the locker room without naming his pitcher. His normal procedure was to stay there until about fifteen minutes before the game, then go through the runway under the stands to the dugout. This time, he came out about half an hour before the game to find all four of his regular starters sitting or standing near their lockers. When he walked toward Parnell, the others stiffened.

"Sorry, kid," McCarthy said in a low voice. "It's the right-hander."

Parnell looked at Dobson, his nearest neighbor.

"Not Dobson," McCarthy said aloud. "Galehouse."

And while eighteen-game-winner Kramer, sixteen-game-winner Dobson, fifteen-game-winner Parnell, and ten-game-winner Kinder stared in disbelief, McCarthy sent the clubhouse boy to get Denny Galehouse, who was shagging flies in the outfield.

A journeyman pitcher who had never enjoyed a remarkable season, Galehouse was nearing the end of a mediocre career. He was as surprised as everyone else when McCarthy picked him to pitch the most important game of the year. He was also exhausted from roaming the outfield. He went to the locker room to lie down for a few minutes, then went out to warm up in front of a grandstand full of fans wondering what he was doing there.

Later, Dave Egan, the same Boston columnist who specialized in antagonizing Ted Williams, wrote a piece to the effect that McCarthy picked Galehouse because he couldn't get anybody else to do the job. According to Egan, the other pitchers pleaded everything from hangnails to headaches to avoid pitching that day.

"Egan's story was ridiculous," Parnell told me years

later. "Each of us would have given anything to pitch that game. Do you realize what it would have meant to the guy who beat the Indians and won the pennant? Besides the World Series loot, he'd pick up a contract for 1949—maybe a multi-year contract, for God knows how much more dough than he'd been getting. Egan dreamed the whole story up. None of us tried to get out of pitching that playoff game. I'd pitched the day before, but I was dying to go out there again."

"Why did McCarthy pick Galehouse?" I asked.

"Beats me," Parnell said. "Denny had once done a great relief job against the Indians. Maybe that was why. But a game with everything riding on it? Doesn't make sense."

Perhaps with the inspiration and bat provided by Manager Lou Boudreau, Cleveland would have beaten anyone that day, but Galehouse made it easy. Before the afternoon was over, Boudreau had a perfect day, with two homers, two singles, and a walk in five trips to the plate. And so while Bearden held the Red Sox to a total of five hits, Boudreau capped off a dream season by leading his club to an 8–3 victory. It was Boudreau's game, Boudreau's pennant, Boudreau's season—one of those unusual years when one man dominated baseball.

Boudreau's great day set him up for a future in Boston, a bonus that paid off a few years later. Sitting in his box atop the roof that day, Tom Yawkey marveled at the play of the thirty-three-year-old Cleveland manager-shortstop. He determined to bring Boudreau to Boston, hoping to infect his all too complacent team with the Boudreau fire and will to win.

In the meantime, Yawkey still had the peerless Mc-

Carthy as a managerial weapon for 1949. Some weapon!
For the second straight year, the best team in baseball got
off to a wheezing, stuttering start. Once again, the boys
who figured to walk away with the pennant were far behind at the end of May—twelve games this time. And after
they finally got on the track toward the top, it took them
over three months to make it.

From early August on, Red Sox players led the American League in every category, while the club gradually
pulled up from its huge deficit to even terms with the
Yankees. Junior Stephens and Ted Williams were one-two
in RBIs, Dom DiMaggio and Johnny Pesky one-two in hits,
Williams and Stephens one-two in home runs.

On August 6, DiMaggio and Williams were first and second in batting; DiMaggio, having safely hit in his thirty-
third straight game, had the most impressive streak going
since his brother Joe had set the record of fifty-six in 1941.
On August 9, Dom's streak ended at thirty-four against
the Yankees, the last club to have held him hitless. He had
begun June 30, hit safely every July game, and continued
through the first week in August. Even after the streak
ended he kept right on hitting for one of the best seasons
of his life.

The Red Sox continued to creep up until they were only
one and a half games behind the Yankees on Labor Day.
At that point Williams led the league in batting, runs, hits,
and homers, with DiMaggio second in hits, Stephens second in home runs, Stephens and Williams one-two in
RBIs, and Kinder and Parnell one-two in pitching. Baseball fans all over the country wondered how such a ball
club still trailed the Yankees, a team which had been

plagued with injuries all year. With Kinder or Parnell pitching, the Red Sox had just about the best man in the league at every single position. Goodman, Doerr, Stephens, Pesky, Williams, DiMaggio, Zarilla, and Tebbetts. It was a dream ball club, which opened the season with one nightmare and was now dashing madly toward another at the close.

When they won two straight over the Yankees to tie for the top in late September, it looked as if they were in. The second game, on September 26, was their last at home, giving them sixty-one victories in seventy-seven games there. That was Parnell's twenty-fifth win of the season and the day Williams hit his forty-third home run. Both Red Sox and Yankees had six games left to play, but Boston was in a much better position, since three of their games would be in Washington against the lowly Senators. And the last two games were against the Yankees on the final weekend of the season. On top of that, the Red Sox rode out of Boston on the wings of a nine-game winning streak.

On September 27, Kramer, in relief of Kinder, beat the Yankees, giving Boston a one-game lead. The next day, Boston won over Washington for their eleventh straight, while the Yankees beat the Athletics. But the day following, the clubs were tied again when the Sox lost to the Senators as the Yankees won.

The Red Sox then went into a dismal batting slump. Despite that, they beat the Senators on Friday, September 30, with five hits, and when the Yanks lost to the A's, moved back into a one-game lead, with two games to go, both in New York. When Allie Reynolds of the Yankees held them to four hits for a 5–4 victory in the Saturday game, the two clubs were back in a top tie, with everything riding on the final game of the season on Sunday, October 2, at Yankee Stadium.

Over 68,000 people, about 10,000 of whom must have come from Boston, jammed the massive ball park for the payoff game. For the second year in a row, the Red Sox were down to the last day and for the second year in a row, Joe McCarthy's strategy, such as it was, exploded in his face.

He started Ellis Kinder against Vic Raschi, New York's only twenty-game winner. Except for a tainted Yankee run in the first inning (Ted Williams misplayed Phil Rizzuto's leadoff hit into a triple and Rizzuto later scored), Kinder held the Yanks scoreless for seven innings, during which they nicked him for only four hits. But the Red Sox could do nothing against Raschi either, and when they came up in the eighth, New York was clinging to a 1–0 lead. But Raschi was obviously laboring, while Kinder, always at his best in clutches, seemed to be getting stronger.

It was here that McCarthy once again exercised his prerogative. Instead of letting Kinder, a good hitter, bat for himself, McCarthy yanked him for a nondescript pinch-hitter named Clyde Wright, who did nothing, and the Red Sox had to go to the bullpen for the Yankee half of the eighth.

Next Parnell, who had pitched only a day or two earlier, came in, another percentage move by McCarthy. "When you want to win," he always said, "go with your best." Parnell was Boston's best pitcher, all right, but starting pitchers usually make poor relievers, especially when they need rest. The young southpaw was no exception.

In the Yankee eighth, Tommy Henrich greeted him with a home run, and Yogi Berra followed with a single. Out came Parnell, to be replaced by Tex Hughson. The Yankees murdered the sore-armed right-hander, winding up with four runs, and Raschi went out to pitch the ninth on a five-run cushion.

He needed nearly all of it. Bobby Doerr, the only Red Sox hitter who hadn't gone into a slump, belted a homer, and the team scored three runs. But it was too late, and the Yankees won a 5–3 victory.

Kinder never got over it. He boiled in the locker room after the game, boiled in the team bus to the airport, boiled in the plane, and then boiled every time he was reminded of the incident. Seven years later, when I saw him at spring training with the Cardinals in St. Petersburg, he exploded again when I mentioned it.

"Goddamit," he said, "if the old man had let me bat for myself that day we'd have won the pennant."

He and Sam Mele were about the only two men on the team who didn't proclaim to the world that McCarthy was the greatest manager they'd ever played for.

The 1950 club was as hotly favored to win as the three previous Red Sox teams, but McCarthy didn't last much beyond Mother's Day. Dismissed at that point, he went home to his farm near Buffalo and was replaced by Steve O'Neill, one of his coaches. O'Neill was a fat, jolly, friendly veteran who had won the 1945 Series with the Tigers.

The last thing the Red Sox needed at that point was a fat, jolly, friendly manager. Despite two blown pennants, the club was loaded with stars who made so much money in the normal course of events that it didn't much matter whether they won or lost. There were thirteen Cadillacs in the players' parking lot, and no fat, jolly, friendly manager was going to mold the owners of those cars into a fighting squadron of perpetual champions.

This attitude was only one of O'Neill's problems. The Boston press, angry over a complete locker room ban before games and a half-hour post-game ban, was constantly pecking away at the whole organization. A defiant Ted Williams continued to proclaim the greatness of Joe McCarthy, while privately referring to the genial O'Neill as a guy who "spent forty years in baseball without learning a thing."

O'Neill was sitting on the hottest seat in baseball. The Red Sox were still considered the best team going, and the feeling was that anybody could win a pennant with them. The 1950 club not only didn't win the pennant, they couldn't even finish second. They trailed both the pennant-winning Yankees and the Tigers, coming home in third place.

To add to O'Neill's woes, Lou Boudreau, after being fired as the Indians' manager, signed a *player's* contract with the Red Sox in November. When that was announced, the experts quickly handed Boudreau a ticket into O'Neill's office, some even predicting that O'Neill wouldn't last out the 1951 season. And truly, nothing was as sure as death, taxes, and Boudreau's inheriting O'Neill's job sooner or later. The only thing that could save his job in 1951 was a pennant, but the men who had failed to win in 1948 and 1949 weren't getting any younger.

Furthermore, Birdie Tebbetts, the only competent catcher on the club, talked himself right off it by telling an audience at his bachelor dinner that the 1949 pitching staff had too many "juvenile delinquents" to win anything. The Red Sox, on orders from Yawkey, sold Tebbetts to Cleveland.

O'Neill did last out the 1951 season, but when the club again finished third, the handwriting on the wall became clearer. While the front office kept denying it, the experts kept predicting Boudreau's promotion from part-time shortstop to full-time manager. One day in October a Boston columnist wrote that Boudreau "positively" had the job. That afternoon the Red Sox issued a denial. The next morning they introduced Boudreau as the new manager for 1952.

It was all done so clumsily that even the straight faces of the front office gang were unconvincing. Boudreau himself met the press with big smiles and the natural charm that had always made him popular with writers. Yes, the Red Sox were going to develop a will to win. Yes, there were too many Cadillacs in the parking lot and too few pennants on the flagpole. No, there won't be any more complacency. No, the complacent men won't be with the ball club long. Yes, everyone will obey the rules or face fines. And so forth.

But Boudreau had his own troubles, because he was Tom Yawkey's personal choice for the job. The rest of the Red Sox brass had been grooming Mike Higgins, who'd been moving up through the minor-league system. Boudreau might trip, but couldn't fall, because if he did he would flop right out of the Red Sox picture.

One bad break for Boston turned out to be a good one for Boudreau. After playing six games in 1952, Ted Williams, a member of the Marine Corps Reserve, was called back into service for the Korean War. Without Williams, the Red Sox were dead; they finished sixth. To make sure no one would hold Boudreau responsible, Yawkey gave him a two-year contract. He lasted through the 1954 season without distinction, finishing fourth both times. Williams didn't get back until early August of 1953 and played only 117 games the following year because of a spring training injury. But by then nothing could save Boudreau. As expected, he was succeeded by Mike Higgins, who had waited patiently in the wings for three years.

Higgins entered like a lion and departed like a lamb. A manager along the lines of McCarthy without the Broadway overtones, he was a patient, plodding, friendly man. In 1955 and 1956 his teams finished fourth, and in 1957 and 1958 he got them up to third place. But by then Williams was nearly through, and the great stars of the late forties were gone. Boston's collapse was not entirely Higgins's fault, nor were many of the other sad events of the next few years.

Higgins was Cronin's last managerial choice, because in 1959 Cronin became president of the American League. His record as general manager was a poor one; McCarthy, the nonmanager, blew two pennants he should have won. O'Neill in his own way also proved to be a nonmanager. He lacked fire and the ability to instill the so necessary will to win. But he was beaten before he started; by the time he took over, the team was so complacent it would have taken a gunslinger to awaken it. Boudreau hadn't been Cronin's choice. Higgins was all right for a few years, except his managerial philosophy was too much like Mc-

Carthy's. He believed in picking the eight best regulars, rotating the best pitchers, and then letting them either win or lose on their own. But where the other Cronin managers had the club at its best, Higgins's teams were full of holes in key positions.

With Cronin gone, Yawkey had an opportunity to appoint a strong general manager who might bring the ball club back to the peak it had reached in the late forties. Instead, he handed the job to Bucky Harris who, like Cronin, was too nice a guy to run a big-league team from the top. Furthermore, he had come to the Red Sox in fulfillment of an old promise, not because he was a capable executive. And after all the bumbling and fumbling of the previous fifteen years, the Red Sox needed a good executive far more than Tom Yawkey needed an old friend. Giving Harris a job was one thing, but making him general manager was a monumental blunder.

With the 1959 Red Sox going nowhere, Harris replaced Higgins with an old friend, Billy Jurges, who took over the club in midseason. There was nothing wrong with this as an interim appointment, which everyone thought it was. But Jurges, a good shortstop in his time, was a hopeless manager, which he quickly proved to everyone except Harris. The club finished fifth, and by the end of the season Jurges, who had never managed in the majors and never did again after leaving Boston, was a nervous wreck.

Waiting in the wings was Gene Mauch, the brightest young manager in baseball. For two years he had piloted Minneapolis, Boston's top farm team, with such distinction that several big-league clubs had already tried to get him. Assured by Cronin that the Red Sox job would even-

On February 25, 1933, the announcement that 30-year-old millionaire Thomas A. Yawkey had purchased the Red Sox was made at the Copley Plaza Hotel in Boston. Left to right: Marty McManus, manager of the team; Bob Quinn, former owner; Yawkey; Eddie Collins, vice-president and general manager; William Harridge, President of the American League; and Fred DeFoe, attorney for Yawkey.

RIGHT: *Ted Williams in 1941, the year he led the American League with a .406 batting average.*

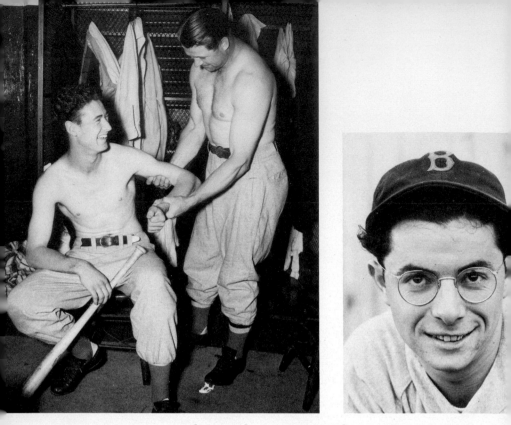

LEFT: *Jimmy Foxx searches for the source of Ted's power. 1941* RIGHT: *Who's better than his brother Joe? Dominic DiMaggio. 1940*

Harry Truman throws out the first ball to open the 1946 season.

Williams with Boston's young shortstop and manager, Joe Cronin. 1941

ABOVE: *Three whose sticks were hot on May 10, 1946, just before the Red Sox met the Yankees in a series at the Stadium. Ted Williams (.424), Johnny Pesky (.427), and Dom DiMaggio (.386).*

BELOW LEFT: *Dave (Boo) Ferriss* RIGHT: *Cecil (Tex) Hughson*

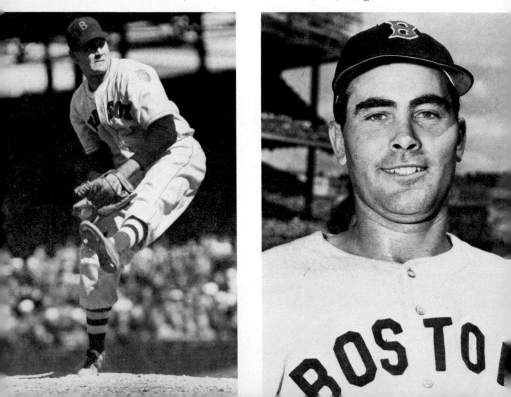

ABOVE: *Tom Yawkey and Joe Cronin scout their future opponent in the 1946 World Series at the second playoff game between the Dodgers and the Cardinals.* BELOW: *The entire Cardinal defense with the exception of the shortstop and left fielder swung sharply to the right when Ted Williams came to bat for the first time in the 1946 World Series opener at Sportsman's Park.*

ABOVE: *Joe McCarthy addresses a somewhat attentive audience as the 1948 training season opens at Sarasota, Florida.*

LEFT: *Mel Parnell. 1949*

Joe McCarthy (LEFT) talks to Jack Kramer, Mickey Harris, Earl Johnson, and Dave Ferriss. Again at Sarasota. 1949

Doerr to Stephens to Goodman erases Yogi Berra of the Yanks. 1949

Beating New York is always cause for happiness. Left to right: Vern Stephens, Al Zarilla, Bobby Doerr, and Johnny Pesky. 1949

A trio of home run hitters on June 8, 1950. Ted Williams (14), Vern Stephens, (11), and the sensational rookie Walt Dropo (11).

LEFT: *Ted in Korea. 1952* RIGHT: *Ted at bat. 1955*

Yogi Berra makes the tag.

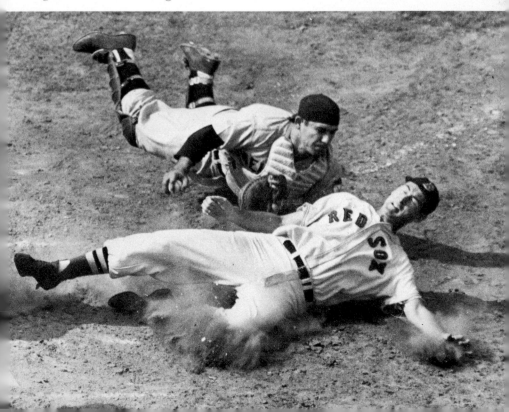

Williams goes up against the Wall. 1958

LEFT: *T.A. and friend.*

BELOW: *Frank Malzone. 1960*

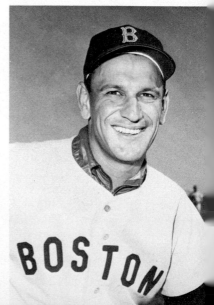

E.J. (Pumpsie) Green

Carl (Yaz) Yastrzemski

Earl Wilson with catcher Bob Tillman after Earl's 1962
no-hitter against the Los Angeles Angels.

ABOVE: *Yaz is safe at the plate against Baltimore. 1972*

LEFT: *Yaz vs. the Wall. 1967*

LEFT: *Jim Lonborg bears down in the 1967 World Series.*

BELOW: *T.A. and friend. 1967*

LEFT: *Dick Williams. 1967*

BELOW: *Lonborg is congratulated by Jay Foy and Elston Howard after he beat the Cardinals in the fifth game of the World Series. 1967*

ABOVE: *Reggie Smith connects.*

RIGHT: *Reggie relaxes.*

Eddie Kasko relieves Jim Lonborg in a game against the Kansas City Royals on June 1, 1971.

Tom Yawkey looks ahead. 1972

tually be his, he turned everything else down. After Cronin left, Mauch, along with most other observers, thought Harris had appointed Jurges only to finish out the 1959 season.

Unhappily for the Fenway faithful, it wasn't so. Harris reappointed Jurges for 1960, to the surprise of Mauch and everyone else, and the disgusted Mauch accepted an offer to manage the Phillies. To make matters worse, Jurges, who was temperamentally unsuited to the pressures of his job, departed during the summer. With nobody else on the horizon, Yawkey gave the job back to Higgins, who had remained with the organization as a sort of superscout.

This was the beginning of a new Red Sox era, as frustrating as any during Yawkey's stewardship—the era of Mike Higgins. The club, handicapped by problems in the front office, sank lower and lower; Higgins nonmanaged it to seventh place in 1960, sixth in 1961, and eighth (in a ten-club league) in 1962.

Obviously, something had to be done. Harris either fell or was pushed out of the front office, and Yawkey moved a reluctant Higgins upstairs to take his place. Higgins, who never wanted to do anything but manage, now found himself general manager of an utterly loused-up organization.

Perhaps the situation would have been a little better if Higgins had named his own successor in the dugout; however, if given that choice, he would have resigned as GM and reappointed himself. He never got that option because Yawkey named Johnny Pesky as manager, which was an excellent appointment. Pesky, always a popular local figure, still made his home in Boston while managing in the minors all over the country. His record was good, and because he had been handling the top Fenway farm club, which had been moved to Seattle, he knew the younger players. Old Red Sox hands sat back with more confidence than they had had in years and hoped that at last the ball club was on the right track.

The 1963 season began as if the Red Sox were going all the way. The club was young and enthusiastic, with a coming superstar in Carl Yastrzemski, older men like shortstop Eddie Bressoud and third baseman Frank Malzone as stabilizing influences, and a good young pitching staff backed by Dick Radatz, the best relief pitcher in baseball that year. By the end of June, Pesky had this crew two games out of first place and talking pennant.

Then, for no apparent reason, the roof fell in. As Yastrzemski later described it: ". . . the collapse was total, with everyone bickering, criticizing, blaming others for his own shortcomings, falling back into deadly cliques. Pesky, who had been the architect of our new-found spirit, practically lost control of the ball club."

Pesky's loss of control was aggravated by Higgins's attitude toward him. The man who didn't want to be general manager barely spoke to his might-have-been-successful manager. This lack of communication between the front office and the locker room simply added fuel to the flames. As the ball club dropped to seventh, Higgins seemed unwilling to make a move to help. And by the end of the season, the only scrap salvaged from this hopeless situation was Yastrzemski's first league batting championship.

Despite the disaster, Pesky came back as manager in 1964, but there was little he could do. Just before the season ended, he was replaced by Billy Herman. Herman had

been a coach under Higgins and was held over at Higgins's
insistence, although Pesky would have preferred to name
his own coaches.

All Herman had in his favor was Higgins's blessing. He
was worse than Pesky, because he was more interested in
golf than in baseball. A two-handicap player, he carried his
clubs wherever he went and played as much as he could,
while telling his players: "You'd better bust your butts for
me or else." Except he had no alternative when they didn't
bust their butts.

Herman lasted two years, and the Red Sox finished ninth
both times. He was, in fact, the last in a long series of bad
managers. A year after Dick O'Connell succeeded Higgins
in the front office, Dick Williams was appointed manager.
When he was so unexpectedly fired, his successor, Eddie
Kasko, moved in with two strikes against him. Those who
felt that Williams had been given a raw deal jumped all
over Kasko. But at this writing he has clung to the job for
three years, while the club's personnel has changed so
drastically that no one is yet sure whether its failure to
repeat the 1967 miracle was Kasko's fault or not.

Even if Kasko succeeds in overcoming his inherited
handicaps, certain fans and observers will always put the
slug on him. Blaming managers for failure, whether they
are responsible or not, is a regional disease of the millions
of people in the northeast corridor and the Maritime Provinces who still live or die with the Red Sox.

The manager's job has been a hot seat ever since Mc-
Carthy's time. And it's doubtful this will change much as
long as big-league baseball is played in Boston. At best, the
position is an unenviable one. Because handling it properly

requires a strong man who has the guts to defy the front office and the luck to win consistently. The only man since World War II who proved he could do this was Dick Williams. The rest, except perhaps Kasko, have been unfortunate, inefficient, inconsistent, or complacent.

It's a thankless job, but it pays well. The fact that so many men have tried it and failed is certainly one of the big problems the Red Sox have faced in the last quarter century. And the manager problem must rank high on the list of what's wrong with the ball club.

CHAPTER 6

The Front Office

There is no nicer guy in or out of baseball than Tom Yawkey: no more loyal friend and no one with a more sincere feeling of good will toward his fellow man. As he told me in the summer of 1972, he has always tried to practice a principle he was brought up to believe in as a special obligation for those born to wealth—to treat human beings as human beings.

Others may have been brought up on the same principle, but few men practice it as faithfully as Tom Yawkey. His trouble is that he is too friendly, too generous and kind. A man with few close friends, he has mixed his personal life very closely with his business life. This is a dangerous practice, and the consequences of it have been felt from the top of the Red Sox organization all the way down to the locker room.

Yawkey's devotion to his own Golden Rule has been partly responsible for the frequent undoing of his ball club. I don't mean that he is wrong—how can you consider a man with such a philosophy wrong? But because of it he has left himself wide open as a potential fall guy for the people he trusts most. He feels that if he treats others with consideration, they will treat him in kind. Some have, but too many others haven't.

No one in baseball has more scars on his feeding hand. Though not all have been inflicted on purpose. In fact, he has received some of his deepest spiritual wounds from men who were acting with the best intentions, hardly aware of the harm they were doing.

A casual, down-to-earth man of good will—especially in this day when everyone wants all they can get for as little as possible—is the last person to run a professional baseball outfit. Such a man is a sitting duck for the selfish, the greedy, and the incompetent, and he is doomed to failure unless he is very lucky. As far as the Red Sox are concerned, Yawkey is not generally lucky. And his luck has not been helped by the fact that for nearly thirty-five years, Yawkey ran his empire on cronyism.

If it is a question of hurting a friend or hurting the ball club, Yawkey has usually hurt the club. Not intentionally, of course. His dearest wish is for a world championship, which he has never won. (Both pennant-winning teams lost the Series to the Cardinals.) His next dearest wish is for a succession of pennants, or at least two back to back or close together. It was thirteen years before he saw his first pennant, and twenty-one more before he saw his next. God only knows if he will get to see another. He was seventy in February of 1973.

"I suppose I'm too sentimental," he told me. "And I guess perhaps I'm too much in favor of the ballplayer."

That was one of the understatements of the century.

Yawkey's sentimentality and partiality to ballplayers go so far that, when I mentioned the players' strike that delayed the start of the 1972 baseball season, he said, "Why blame the players? They have rights, too."

I doubt if any other owner or executive in baseball felt the same way. The strike was caused by a deep chasm between players and owners which, at that time, couldn't be bridged. It finally ended in compromise, as most strikes must. But if the settlement had been left up to Yawkey, the players would have been given everything they demanded, because he is and always has been for them, even at his own expense.

Yawkey has had some personal friends among his ballplayers, but that is not the cronyism which has hurt him most. The big problem has been his close association with the men he has entrusted to run his ball club.

The first was Eddie Collins. Yawkey was very fortunate in that choice, for Collins was as good an executive as he had been a ballplayer. It is significant that he was never popular with the writers or players; he was too busy running the organization, which he did with great efficiency. Because he was old enough to be Yawkey's father and had been idolized by Yawkey since he was a boy, Collins could do what he pleased with the club. That he pleased to run it properly and was capable of doing so, was a great break for Yawkey.

The club that ran away with the 1946 pennant was Collins's, built up through outstanding minor-league purchases, shrewd trades, and the development of an effective farm system. Hughson, Harris, and Ferriss came out of that farm system. Williams, Doerr, and DiMaggio were bought from the Pacific Coast League clubs that had originally signed them. The rest of the regulars came in trades or purchases from established teams, as did Joe Cronin, the manager.

Collins not only ran the Red Sox with an iron hand, he also selected only those people he thought were qualified for their jobs. Cronyism never played a part in any of his choices. He demanded good people, insisted on high performance, kept a rein on Yawkey's checkbook in paying salaries, and conducted the club's business as it should be conducted. For this reason Collins made enemies, but he didn't care. His job was to give the Red Sox the best possible management, and he didn't worry about ruffled feelings along the way.

But even if Collins hadn't had executive ability, he would have been general manager indefinitely, because Yawkey liked and admired him so much. This was also true of Cronin. When the ailing Collins could no longer function as boss of the organization, Yawkey replaced him with another man he had admired as a ballplayer and liked as a friend. Yawkey knew as little about Cronin's executive abilities as he had about Collins's qualifications. It was pure lucky accident that Collins turned out to be a good general manager, and pure unlucky accident that Cronin turned out to be a poor one.

Yawkey and Cronin had become close friends long before Yawkey appointed him general manager. By then it was unthinkable to him to name anyone else. He should have gone outside the organization, if necessary, to find someone as well qualified as Collins. But that would have meant hurting a friend, which Yawkey couldn't do.

Cronin was a poor choice because he too surrounded himself with friends in key jobs, and the club suffered. He made Johnny Murphy the farm director, for example. Murphy, a great relief pitcher under Joe McCarthy with the Yankees, was not a good farm director for the Red Sox. But Cronin wouldn't fire Murphy for the same reason Yawkey wouldn't fire Cronin. Murphy was his friend, a good guy, and Cronin couldn't fire a friend.

Long before Cronin became general manager, he carried enough weight with Yawkey to get his friend, Ed Doherty, a job as the first Red Sox press agent. Friendship was Doherty's only qualification for the job, except for a few years' experience as a composing room makeup man with one of the Providence newspapers. Composing room make-up men do not get around, which is just what a good press agent must do. But Doherty was Cronin's friend, and that was good enough for Yawkey. Collins could have stopped the appointment, but he didn't know or care enough about press relations to interfere. As it turned out, Doherty did a terrible job, because his idea of good public relations, to quote Dave Egan, was "a punch in the nose if you don't agree with him."

Whether it was Murphy's fault or Cronin's, the club at one point had the biggest collection of useless scouts in baseball. The front office kept adding to the staff without subtracting from it. I doubt if a single scout was fired during Cronin's tenure as general manager. Three or four were friends from his days as a rookie shortstop with Pittsburgh. A job as Red Sox scout was a ticket to permanent employment.

At one point, half a dozen scouts were working out of

the Boston office. A couple were outstanding, but the rest were deadwood, with the result that the Braves, with only one New England scout, annually signed more good ballplayers from there than all the Red Sox scouts combined.

There was never any real delegation of authority. The best executive in the place was Dick O'Connell, the business manager. He was left alone because nobody else knew or worried about the job. O'Connell was originally hired as general manager of one of the farm clubs, and he did so well that he was promoted—one of the few front office men to get his job on ability alone.

All through the fifties the club became worse and worse, yet Yawkey couldn't fire his friend Cronin. It took him years to see that the team's troubles began at the top, and even then he would not act until he was sure Cronin was taken care of. This has always been a Yawkey practice, born, like so many of his habits, of sheer decency. His friend Cronin was doing a poor job as general manager, but he could not simply be dumped. He had to go out with pride, preferably to a job which would insure his financial comfort for as long as he lived.

In 1958, Will Harridge, who had served four seven-year terms as president of the American League, announced his impending retirement. The league presidency is whatever the man in office makes it. It can be a figurehead job, with no authority except to appoint umpires and rubber-stamp other people's decisions, or it can be a job of great weight and influence. Club owners naturally prefer a figurehead, and Cronin had all the earmarks. He was a nice guy with a big smile and a ready handshake, and he was a member of the old school which preached the great goodness of America's national pastime. It was helpful that he also happened to be a Hall of Fame shortstop. No former star had ever been president of either league. Cronin's name would add prestige to the office. When Yawkey either suggested it or arranged for someone else to suggest it, there wasn't a single dissenting vote.

Cronin left the Red Sox organization in a shambles, and Bucky Harris, his successor, did nothing to improve the situation. Harris, in fact, cost the Red Sox their spring training base in Sarasota. Cronin had been after the city fathers for several years to improve the ball park, which had antiquated stands, locker room, and press facilities. Before leaving, Cronin had arranged for the team to train in Scottsdale, Arizona, in the spring of 1959, but this was not intended to be permanent. Cronin figured that Sarasota would fix up the park, and the team could return the following year.

But by the time the Red Sox went to Arizona, Cronin was American League president and Harris was in charge of the ball club. Sarasota, which had no team training there in 1959, spruced up the park and the Red Sox might have returned in 1960. But, once in Scottsdale, Harris signed a long-term contract for the team to train there. In the meantime, the White Sox, who weren't happy in Tampa, where they had trained for some years, moved to Sarasota, where they have been ever since.

In the seven years the Red Sox trained at Scottsdale, they lost contact with a great many fans who had followed them to Florida, but either wouldn't or couldn't go to Arizona. The hottest adult fans a ball club has are those who see them in spring training, where everyone is relaxed, and contact between players and fans is easy. The Red Sox finally returned to Florida, setting up spring training in Winter Haven, where they are now gradually winning new fans and reclaiming some of the old.

But that long hiatus from Florida was due to Bucky Harris's short-sightedness in not leaving the door open to return there quickly. As a matter of fact, Harris did nothing of any consequence in the two years he was general manager except be a nice guy. Yawkey finally let him go, perhaps the first time he ever fired a friend, and for two years the Red Sox got along without a general manager.

Mike Higgins, who took over the job in 1963, was no better able to handle it than either Harris or Cronin. Once again, Yawkey let his heart rule his head. Higgins was his friend; he needed a general manager. Putting the two together was the simplest thing to do, and Yawkey did it.

Higgins butchered the job through inaction. He tried to run the front office as he had tried to run the ball club: from the bench, with equally disastrous results. The old McCarthy theory that a ball club will reach its rightful level if left alone works only when the club is basically sound. The teams Higgins had managed were basically lousy and, left alone, just kept getting worse.

The same was true when Higgins, having won a reputation for patience (translation: procrastination), made no move to improve the front office. He couldn't, because he didn't know how. The only two solid areas, the results of changes Yawkey had made before Higgins took over, were the business department and the farm system.

The business office was run, as it had been for some years, by Dick O'Connell. After Harris was fired, O'Connell took on more and more responsibilities until he became a sort of all-around troubleshooter. And when Higgins turned out to be as inept as his immediate predecessors, O'Connell assumed some of his duties, too.

In 1960, after it became apparent that Harris was in over his head as general manager, Yawkey had fired John Murphy (Cronin's friend, not Yawkey's) as farm director and replaced him with Neil Mahoney, the supervisor of scouts. Mahoney was as competent in his job as O'Connell in his. He cleaned out the deadwood, sliced the scouting staff almost in half, and within a few years was supplying the Red Sox with an increasing number of good ballplayers.

Besides his appointment of Eddie Collins, Yawkey's best moves were putting more and more responsibility on O'Connell's shoulders and making Mahoney the farm director. Both men had earned their new jobs in their own offices, not in Yawkey's private suite. Both had worked years for Yawkey, but neither was a special friend. They were simply competent men who knew what they were doing.

Which was more than could be said for Higgins. He was the last example of Yawkey cronyism. Some time between 1961 and 1965, Yawkey finally learned the futility of that system. The lesson came hard, but was inevitable. Never in the years of Yawkey's ownership had the ball club been so bad for so long. It finished seventh in 1960, sixth in 1961, eighth in 1962, seventh in 1963, eighth in 1964, and ninth in 1965. Not even during World War II, when they sandwiched a fourth place between two seventh-place finishes, had the Red Sox been that consistently horrible under Yawkey.

The club really hit bottom in 1965, with Higgins floundering around as general manager and Billy Herman, the manager, losing more sleep over his golf score than his ball club. Herman, having failed to make any of his charges bust their butts for him, sat contentedly on a two-year contract given him by his pal Higgins at the start of the season. No matter what happened in 1965, Herman was all set for two years, during which he would make enough money to buy a lifetime supply of golf balls.

Club morale was at its worst, although several ballplayers were collecting a king's ransom. And prospects for the future seemed bleak, despite good young material coming up through the farm system. Somewhere along the line, the young players were still being mishandled, although Mahoney was trying to correct this situation. And the good natural players who finally reached the Red Sox were being royally mishandled by Herman. The most flagrant examples were Rico Petrocelli and Jim Lonborg, who came up together in 1965. Petrocelli, a timid, insecure young man plagued with minor injuries, got nothing but abuse from the manager. And Lonborg, who had great natural ability but needed help, was getting none. These two, along with Tony Conigliaro, who had come up the year before, were the first of the talented kids who later helped make the 1967 Impossible Dream come true.

But there would not have been an Impossible Dream team with Higgins in the front office or Herman on the bench, and at last Yawkey recognized it. In September of 1965, with the team anchored in ninth place and sure to finish there, Yawkey fired a friend for the last time and replaced him with an executive. Dick O'Connell succeeded Mike Higgins as general manager.

The era of cronyism, of jolly good fellowship, of heart

ruling head, was over. The Red Sox were finally a going concern, run by an experienced executive who did not and never has hired men to handle key jobs simply because they were his friends.

CHAPTER 7

Press Relations

Relations between the Red Sox and the Boston press were excellent during the first few years of Tom Yawkey's ownership, and they are again today. But for a long time between the old days and the present, the situation was very bad, to the point that today's baseball press in Boston takes a rap earned largely by its predecessors.

The rap was well earned. It has often been said that one reason for the long deterioration in club-press relations was the tremendous size of the Boston press. Size may have had an effect, but the press corps is bigger than ever now, and the old wounds between writers and ball club have long since healed.

No, the size of the press wasn't the primary problem. When Yawkey bought the Red Sox, the team was covered by one man from each of the nine Boston papers. But in those days no writers went anywhere with the club except to spring training, and few ever went into the locker rooms during the regular season.

As the team improved, the daily newspapers began assigning writers to travel with them. But—and this is very important in understanding the history of Red Sox press relations—the club paid the writers' traveling expenses, including train fare, hotel and food bills, liquor, and incidentals. This was standard practice with most of the big-league teams, with the result that the newspapers were under heavy obligation to clubs everywhere.

In effect, ball clubs were buying the newspapers' good will by sheer bribery. In return for paying expenses, the clubs expected, and got, a good press. In two-team towns like Boston, since the Braves also played there, the clubs actually competed with each other for the favor of the press.

Before Yawkey bought the Red Sox, the Boston press was inclined to favor the Braves because they were more generous. Neither club could actually afford this kind of generosity, since the teams weren't much good and didn't draw crowds. But Judge Emil Fuchs, the Braves' president until the mid-thirties, had a sharper sense of public relations than Bob Quinn, who then ran the Red Sox (and sold them to Yawkey). Fuchs plied the press with food and liquor, played customers' bridge with favored sports editors and columnists, and gave the writers better Christmas gifts. This was known as "class" (it actually was more effective bribery), and to their dying day, some veteran Boston baseball writers stoutly insisted that the Braves had more class than the Red Sox.

When Yawkey came along, it turned into an uphill battle for the Braves. Fuchs was going broke, but even if he weren't, he couldn't have competed with Yawkey who had plenty of money to spend. Some of that money, of course, was earmarked for entertainment of the press.

Since nobody had traveled with either team for years, it was an innovation when the Boston papers began sending men on the road with the Red Sox. In general, the papers continued to get their out-of-town stories on the Braves from local papers in the cities where they played, but Fuchs gamely offered to pay the expenses of any Boston writer who traveled with his club. A few did, but it was just a courtesy, although a pretty expensive one for the ball club. The Fuchs Braves finally went broke in 1935, and eventually Quinn got together another syndicate and bought them.

By 1938 the Red Sox were far the more attractive of the two clubs, but Eddie Collins, always economy-minded, incurred the displeasure of the press by cutting down on their expenses. In accordance with the custom of the times, the Red Sox continued to pay traveling bills and to keep an open bar at Fenway Park, but, because Collins insisted on it, they drew the line there. Writers traveling with the team received the same cash allowances as players. However, the traveling secretary was authorized to take favored writers out for dinner and drinks. (This meant those who never deviated from the club line, plus one or two writers who acted in a semi-executive capacity or as makeup men at home, deciding what and how much copy was to be run in their papers.)

The Braves were more liberal, because Bob Quinn's policy toward the press had changed since he ran the Red Sox. He allowed his traveling secretary to take care of all the press on the road and at home. This contributed to the continued myth that the Braves had more class than the

Red Sox. No question, the Braves were more generous to
the press than the Red Sox.

This resulted in all sorts of distortions by the press. The
Red Sox, although richer than the Braves, had less class.
But the baseball writers favored by the Red Sox thought
they had more class. The class distinction applied as much
to the traveling secretaries as to the ball clubs, although all
they did was spend the organization's money. Thus, Duffy
Lewis, the Braves' traveling secretary, was considered to
have more class than Phil Troy, the traveling secretary of
the Red Sox. Lewis could take anyone out when on the
road, Troy only a favored few.

There were other factors. In an era of train travel, com-
pact leagues, long stands on the road, and little, if any,
night baseball, ballplayers and writers had more chances
to become friendly. Although the writers generally stayed
out of locker rooms (some didn't even visit dugouts before
games), they knew the players better from fraternizing on
trains and in hotel lobbies. This was an added incentive to
the writers to soft-pedal poor playing and protect playboy
athletes. Nobody likes to knock his friends, and to criticize
in print a ballplayer with whom you had been drinking
the night before was considered very dirty pool.

Objective reporting was a myth. All a ballplayer had to
do to be sure of a good press was pick up a bar check once
in a while—the more the better. Some ballplayers, notably
Jimmy Foxx, were famous for having a long arm when the
tab came around. Foxx, a big spender when he could afford
it (he died broke), would never let anyone pay for anything when he was around. He was known to have class
when he played for the Red Sox.

Some ballplayers picked up the check only for certain

writers. A Braves pitcher (who later ran a bar of his own) had one of the Boston writers so deep in his pocket that whenever he was knocked out of the box, the writer hardly mentioned it in his story the next day. For the writer, that pitcher had class.

Thus in Boston there was a tight little island of baseball writers with ten-cent pocketbooks and million-dollar tastes. Forgetting who paid them their salaries, they were more loyal to the ball clubs and selected players than to their own papers. They refused to recognize that their primary job was to inform their readers about what was really going on. All they ever wrote about were the good plays on the field (home team errors were soft-pedaled) or, if there wasn't a game, whatever the ball club wanted them to write. They withheld the juicy stories and wrote only the pap, for which the club paid them in hospitality and expenses.

Because of the gravy and pleasant associations, to say nothing of the hours (afternoons only, plus the time it took to write a game story), baseball writers were second only to columnists in prestige in the sports writing trade. A baseball writing job was considered a real plum. This suited everyone: the ball clubs and players were getting only good publicity, the writers were coddled to death and living very well, and the newspapers got away with paying low salaries and keeping their writers on the road at little or no expense.

I know of one baseball writer who was happy with his eighteen-dollar-a-week salary and positively ecstatic when raised to the thirty-six required by Roosevelt's NRA regulations. His honeymoon was a trip around the baseball circuit for himself and his bride, paid for by the club. I know of dozens of writers who glowingly praised the lackadaisical play of ballplayers exhausted from nights on the town. And I know of dozens more who protected erring ballplayers just because the clubs wanted them to.

This was the baseball press that Tom Yawkey met when he first purchased the Red Sox. He became accustomed to buying good publicity with his own hospitality, which was lavish. And there is no question in my mind that as the years went by he developed a contempt for the press, which I suspect he keeps to this day. This, I'm sure, is why he became so bitter when the press seemingly turned on him and belted the brains out of his ball club and its players.

It all started with Ted Williams, because Williams was the first to show public signs of discontent. Traveling with Williams was no picnic, but he was a lamb compared to Lefty Grove, who replied to questions in grunts and often wouldn't talk to anyone, teammates included. Writers approached Williams prepared for an argument, but it took a brave man to approach Grove, especially after he had lost a tough ball game.

Williams was a needler, clever and funny even when the writer was the object of his disaffection. Grove was just a great pitcher who, if he knew about anything other than baseball or had a gag in his austere system, kept it all very much to himself. He might have been madder at the world than Williams, but since he never showed his anger in public, there was nothing to criticize him for. Baiting him wouldn't have been any fun, because he wouldn't have reacted. Baiting Williams, on the other hand, was a game because Williams played it just as hard as the press. Besides, Williams's faults were right out in the open for everyone to see. Grove only seethed and sulked. Williams blew his stack.

So the man primarily responsible for the troubles the Red Sox had with the press was the needler, not the grouch. The writers of Grove's time protected him from the public eye. Baseball fans knew nothing about Grove beyond what they could see on the field. But every move Williams made, on or off the field, was faithfully reported by somebody, particularly if it was to his detriment. If the writers had been as frank about Grove's peccadillos as about Williams's, Grove's reputation as the Terrible Tempered Mr. Bang would have been so solid that even at his worst Williams couldn't have made a dent in it. As it was, Grove is remembered as a sort of lovable character who overcame great odds to win his three hundredth game in his last year in baseball, and Williams is remembered as a horrible example of what a public figure ought not to be. Good Old Mose! Bad Old Ted!

For three years the two men were teammates and were covered by the same press, which adds to the puzzle of their opposite press treatment. But it was during this period that subtle changes—obvious after World War II but unnoticed before it—were beginning to take place in the baseball press as a whole. Younger, more challenging writers were coming along to plague ballplayers with questions that the athletes had never faced before. The talents of a man in a ball game had once been the only thing that mattered. Now the public, whose interests the new press reflected, had to know more about these performers. Fans could see what was happening on the field or hear about it on the radio. But they wanted to know what made these athletes tick, what went on in the dugout, in the locker room, off the field in public and in private.

Williams was a natural target for the new press. He defied the public, called it names which on a clear day could be heard all over the park, and refused to take lightly the boos, Bronx cheers, or criticism of either fans or writers. Dave Egan and Duke Lake reported his actions with a combination of wry humor and sheer horror. As one incident led to another, the ballplayer and the writers were constantly at each other's throats.

Another important factor was that the Boston press was not only changing but growing. The exclusive little club of baseball writers who could be bought for a meal and a few drinks expanded into a huge group that soon became the next to largest chapter (behind New York) of the Baseball Writers of America. Instead of one man, the papers began sending two or three to cover the Red Sox, who by then were always pennant contenders while their poor relations down the street, the Braves, perpetually rested in the nether regions of their own league.

Although the number of Boston papers had decreased, the number of papers covering the Red Sox increased. Providence and Worcester had covered Boston baseball for years. Now Quincy, Holyoke, Springfield, Lynn, New Bedford, Brockton, Framingham, Lowell, Salem, Manchester, N.H., and a dozen others, including a few foreign-language dailies in the area, were beginning to cover both clubs, with special emphasis on the Red Sox. One of the foreign language papers, *La Notizia*, published in Boston's

North End, got more scoops about Ted Williams than all the other newspapers combined. This was because Williams gleefully gave exclusive stories to *La Notizia's* rotund, huge-beaked, good-natured sports editor, Johnny Garro. Many a Williams story broke in the regular papers days after *La Notizia* had published it in Italian.

The more attention the press paid the Red Sox, the less the Red Sox gave the press. Until the Boston papers began paying their own writers' traveling expenses, sports editors were sometimes at swords' points with the front office over the men covering the ball club. As long as the club paid the writers' expenses, it *did* have some control. When a writer wouldn't conform, the management simply refused to pick up his road tab. More than one who incurred the wrath of the Red Sox was reassigned to the Braves or taken off the baseball beat.

Younger writers were covering the club as it never had been covered before. They haunted the locker rooms and the dugouts, broke stories the old-timers had but didn't dare break, and gave the Boston press a new look while infuriating the teams.

After Egan and Lake pointed out the feet of clay on which, they claimed, Ted Williams ran, he became everybody's favorite target. Soon the newcomers among the press began to find flaws in other ballplayers, too. Baseball, a sacred cow for half a century, lost its last real defense when the newspapers started paying their own way. The older men continued to play the ball club's game from force of habit. Their juniors, who had never enjoyed the benefits the elders had known, liked their jobs because they were fans, but did no hero-worshipping.

Boston's reputation of having a tough press for baseball people to deal with was justified, but it wasn't any worse than the baseball press of several other cities, just bigger. The press in other cities, particularly Cleveland and Detroit, was fully as vitriolic, but no other city had a Ted Williams. Because of his prominence, he was the reason for Boston's reputation as a tough newspaper town. There must have been dozens of stars in previous years who disliked the writers (Ty Cobb was a classic example), but at that time the press never wrote about such things, nor did the players talk about it. But Williams told so many people in so many places how much he hated the Boston press that word of its toughness spread fast. Actually, I doubt if he ever hated the press as much as he claimed. He just liked to watch it squirm like a fish on his hook.

His real hatred was directed at Egan and Lake. Other writers annoyed him periodically, but his general animosity toward them was usually a gigantic put-on, which he enjoyed no end. Although he truly had a frightful temper and a short fuse, some of his tantrums were no more genuine than Victor McLaglen's in *What Price Glory?* Williams, in fact, would have made a great actor.

After his last game before leaving for active duty in the Korean War in May of 1952, the Boston writers presented him with an autographed baseball. He looked at it and grunted, "What the hell do you expect me to do with this bleeping thing?" But he carefully put it in his luggage and later found a place for it among his baseball souvenirs in his Florida home.

Up until World War II, which changed everyone, the struggle between Red Sox and press was only beginning.

The battle lines were drawn, but suddenly more important things than baseball were on the minds of players, the press, and the public. Still the resulting truce was only for the duration. When baseball returned to normal in 1946, even the greatness of that Red Sox team could not cover up the real antagonism developing between press and ballplayers, which erupted the day the pennant was clinched. Individual writers and players got along all right, but as groups, they were like the Hatfields and the McCoys.

The man in control in the locker room was always Williams. It was he who first demanded the locker-room ban which went into effect on opening day in 1950. The ban originally kept all writers out before games and for an hour after games. The announcement of it was greeted in the press box with more amazement than anger. The writers battled it by going to Joe Cronin, the general manager. However, instead of demanding an immediate reversal of the ban, they *asked*. And instead of threatening to boycott the ball club, they subserviently accepted whatever terms they could get.

Cronin said he would do what he could, that the ban had been voted by the ballplayers and that it was their locker room to handle as they pleased. He also said he would talk it over with the manager (Joe McCarthy) to see what could be done. This was all arrant, arrogant nonsense. As general manager of the ball club, Cronin could have ended the ban any time he wanted to. However, the fact that it lasted as long as it did was at least partly the fault of the writers. They didn't fight hard enough against it.

Other clubs had tried variations of locker room bans, but quickly backtracked because the newspapers stuck to-

gether. When ·Leo Durocher managed the Brooklyn
Dodgers, he once threw Dick Young out of the locker room
and told him to stay out. Young did, and so did all the
other members of the New York press. Within twenty-four
hours, the Dodgers, realizing their error, revoked Durocher's order. To my knowledge, they never again tried
to keep the press out of the locker room during the regular
season.

But when the Red Sox banned the entire Boston press,
they got away with it because the Boston papers refused to
get together and hit back. By then, since the *Transcript*
had folded, there were eight papers, plus the others from
nearby cities. The ban stuck because Williams wanted it,
and neither his teammates nor his bosses cared to cross
him. McCarthy approved of it, and Cronin continued to
use the excuse that he had no control over the locker room.
Eventually the one-hour post-game ban was cut to half an
hour for the rest of the 1950 season. Later it was cut to
fifteen minutes, and that rule lasted for years, as did the
pre-game ban.

Nearly twenty years later, when Williams became manager of the Washington Senators, now the Texas Rangers,
he instituted a fifteen-minute post-game press ban. The
Washington press raised hell about it, but Williams was
adamant, and the ban was in effect as long as the team
stayed in Washington.

In 1939, Boston's American League team decided to hire a
press agent, which was an excellent idea, but they couldn't
have chosen a worse first one than Ed Doherty. Doherty,
well aware of Yawkey's years of hospitality toward the
press, considered the writers parasites and made no at-

tempt to conceal his contempt for them. But he never tried to separate the old writers from the new, the men who let themselves be bribed from those who didn't, or the men seeking legitimate stories from those who wanted only to stir up trouble (of which there were astonishingly few). He acted as if his job was to keep writers from doing theirs, and succeeded in making more enemies than friends for the ball club. His standard reply to anything but routine questions was, "How the hell do I know?" At least he was consistent, because he treated everyone alike. His trouble was really lack of knowledge—unless he was acting under orders from his front office bosses. This possibility could not be ruled out.

After World War II, the Red Sox shifted Doherty to another job and for several years got along with a haphazard public relations setup. Neither Yawkey nor Cronin, who still had fuzzy, unrealistic ideas about the press, as well as contempt for it, thought the press warranted an experienced public-relations expert. For a while, the job of press agent was combined with that of traveling secretary. Later, it was turned over to Larry Woodall. An aging supernumerary, Woodall had never concealed his contempt for the press in the days when he was a coach.

This appointment was the supreme insult, for Woodall not only disliked the press, he knew nothing whatever about public relations. His first action each spring was to circulate among the rookies, telling them not to talk to the Boston writers because they couldn't be trusted. As a bridge between the press and the players, he was worse than Doherty. He wouldn't even give out the players' phone numbers to writers looking for feature stories. Only an expert could have reversed the bad situation with the press, and Woodall was far from that.

No one suffered more than the Red Sox themselves from their ridiculous press policy. Writers deliberately went looking for damaging stories, and sports editors made no bones about printing them. The situation was at its worst after the Red Sox blew the 1948 and 1949 pennants, partly because of the arrogance of the front office, partly because of the resentment of the press, and partly because Williams continued to make himself a natural target. As long as ticket sales held up, the club didn't seem to care. They took the line that they didn't need the press, especially since radio and television could, as they saw it, give the public better coverage.

Not until 1954, when attendance really began dropping, did they turn the PR job over to a real newspaperman. When Cronin hired the late Joe McKenney to try to pick up the shattered pieces, it was the first time the Red Sox showed any inclination to recognize the importance of the press. Both McKenney and his successor, Bill Crowley, finally succeeded in giving the press more than hospitality, which Tom Yawkey for years had mistakenly thought was all it wanted. The elaborate press facilities he had built on the roof of the Fenway Park grandstand (they are still among the best in the major leagues, with an open bar before and after games and excellent food brought in by an outside caterer) would have been enough for the old-time writers.

But the newcomers, while they accepted the goodies, did not see the club's hospitality as an important factor at all. These new-breed writers were more interested in facts, figures, and direct contact with ballplayers in order to get the stories they wanted. McKenney, who held the job until he went with Cronin to the American League office as public relations director in 1959, was the first Red Sox press official who tried to help them. McKenney did a good job, and Crowley, a veteran of many facets of public relations, still does a superb one.

Crowley was for several years a member of the radio and television crew that broadcast Red Sox games. In that capacity, he saw the Boston press at its best and at its worst. He knew the writers who covered the ball club and the columnists who, although they didn't concentrate on baseball, wrote reams of copy about it. And he recognized one thing that the brass didn't—that the slipping Red Sox, no longer the most important part of Boston's multi-sports scene, were losing the stranglehold they had once had on New England sports fans. With Williams's retirement, they had to reshape their image, a job that could best be done by the press.

The worst thing that could happen to the ball club was indifference. With Williams gone, the writers, in some ways the club's best fans, were beginning to show signs that they didn't care what happened to the Red Sox. And if the writers didn't care, it wouldn't be long before the public didn't care either. The team was in the middle of an arid period when Crowley became PR director. In order to maintain the interest of the public, Crowley had to keep alive the writers' interest.

There was an unusual complication. By the early sixties, the big man around Fenway Park, aside from Yawkey, was Mike Higgins, managing the club for the second time after the abortive Billy Jurges adventure. Higgins had caused

deep-dyed resentment among the writers because he
played footsie with one in particular. Crowley knew about
this situation when he took over the public relations office.
He had the ticklish job of trying to keep the whole press
happy while one member was getting exclusives from Higgins on the top stories. At best it was an almost impossible
situation.

When Higgins became general manager, he was, in effect, Crowley's boss. But because of his years on the broad-
casting team as well as through earlier contacts, Crowley
had developed a good relationship with Tom Yawkey, without having become a pal. He finally was able to convince
Yawkey that the team needed all the help they could get
from the entire press, not just one individual writer.

This one-man favoritism was one of the factors which
eventually cost Higgins his own job. Yawkey named Johnny
Pesky as new manager the same day he announced Higgins's promotion to the front office, in New York during
the 1962 World Series. The next three years were rough
ones for Crowley, who walked a tightrope between Higgins and his journalistic buddy and the rest of the Boston
press. Despite a tense and worsening relationship with
Higgins, Crowley managed to keep most of the press happy
by announcing all the big stories he could before Higgins
had time to give them exclusively to one man. It wasn't
easy, since Higgins himself was the source of many of
these stories.

Gradually, Crowley won over the confidence of the
press. While visitors from other cities referred periodically
to the toughness of Boston's press, the writers by then were
no problem to Crowley. To this day, in fact, Crowley insists
they never were a problem after Ted Williams retired.

There have been occasional hassles between individual writers and individual players, but none any worse than what happens in other big-league cities.

The most ticklish job Crowley had was controlling the news of Higgins's firing as general manager on September 16, 1965. Positive that the first person Higgins would tell would be his friend, Crowley advised Dick O'Connell, the new general manager, to break the story at a press conference forty-five minutes after the game against Cleveland at Fenway Park that afternoon. If he didn't, Crowley figured, one paper alone would have it, and the Red Sox would have all the other papers down their throats. O'Connell agreed.

When Yawkey personally gave Higgins the bad news about an hour before the game started, Higgins asked that it be held overnight so he could leave town without having to face the press. Yawkey said he would try, but knowing of Higgins's friendship with one writer, refused to make any promises. In the meantime, O'Connell told Crowley that Higgins knew the worst, was leaving during the game, and would probably be on his way home to Dallas by nightfall.

Everything appeared to be under control except for a most unexpected development. By the seventh inning, Dave Morehead, the Red Sox pitcher, had a no-hitter going. But even with this excitement, Crowley had to see that the Higgins story was broken to everyone before the one writer who knew about it could get it into his paper.

So Crowley announced over the press box loudspeaker, "There will be an important announcement forty-five minutes after the game."

It looked as if the Red Sox management was trying to

upstage one of their own pitchers! As Morehead continued to mow down the Indians, Harold Kaese, the able Boston *Globe* columnist, went to Crowley and said, "Do you mean you have something to announce as important as what's happening on the field right now?"

"You'll see when you get there," Crowley said.

When Morehead completed the no-hitter, Yawkey made one of his rare trips to the locker room to congratulate the pitcher and go through a ceremony of tearing up his contract and giving him a raise. He then went up to the press room in time for Crowley's announcement.

Although there was some grumbling over the timing, since it took the spotlight away from Morehead's performance, Crowley had no choice. Since he couldn't explain the reason for the announcement at that precise moment, he didn't try. If I'm not mistaken, this is the first time it ever has been explained.

Although the Boston press is now as reasonable as any other sports press in the country, it still takes a bum rap because of its past reputation. There's no question about one thing, however—its awesome size. At a spring training game against Kansas City in Winter Haven in 1972, the Royals were ridiculously outnumbered in the press box. Twenty-six Boston writers were covering the game, while only one Kansas City writer, Joe McGuff, was present.

"You must feel outnumbered," someone said to McGuff.

"Outnumbered?" he said. "I'm smothered!"

When Boston played Cleveland, Herb Score, the former Indians fireball pitcher who now helps broadcast their games, looked around the press box and said, "My God, you've got more writers than ballplayers." Then he added,

"I don't see how a Red Sox ballplayer can ever say anything before or after games without some writer hearing him."

He was right. With so many writers around, the Red Sox have little privacy. Those who want any privacy have to go hide in the shower. But relations between the ball club and the press are far more peaceful than in Ted Williams's time. There was a time when the writers, if not causing problems, aggravated them. I speak from experience. For three and a half years, ending in late 1968, I wrote a column three times a week for the Boston *Herald Traveler*. I was as bad as any other writer and worse than most.

CHAPTER 8

Integration

The Red Sox were the last team in the major leagues to have a black ballplayer. Whether this was an oversight, failure to find the right man, short-sighted club policy, or deliberate refusal to look has always been a matter of hot argument among fans.

My own conviction is that it was deliberate, but not in the way people think. The problem was not at the top, as many Red Sox fans and observers thought. Yawkey wanted a black ballplayer almost from the beginning, although he never made a big deal of it because he trusted his farm system to sign promising ballplayers, regardless of their color. Cronin made the same mistake. It's possible that even John Murphy, the farm director, was not aware of what was happening within his own department. Murphy, who had no more personal prejudices than Cronin or Yawkey, would have signed a good black ballplayer as soon as his scouts dug one up. But his scouts never seemed able to find one. When they did find one, his so-called superscouts would come back with a poor report on the player. So the real culprits in this highly sensitive area seem to have been some of the individuals within the Red Sox system.

The stock club answer to the obvious question, "Why don't the Red Sox get a black player?" was, "We will when we find a good one." That this was a copout on somebody's part was proved time and again by other big-league clubs, few of whom had trouble finding good black ballplayers. However, the entire American League was well behind the National in this respect. Bill Veeck signed Larry Doby, the first black American Leaguer, for the Indians in 1947, the same year that Jackie Robinson, after a season in the minors, broke in at Brooklyn. The rest of the American League openly dragged its feet, while the National League continued to get more and more outstanding blacks. One result has been that the American is still feeling the effects of its longtime failure to tap the black baseball market when the Negro leagues were full of fine players.

The Yankees, the Tigers, and the Red Sox were the last three big-league clubs to join the human race. The Yankees signed Elston Howard to a minor-league contract in 1950, but didn't bring him up to New York until 1955. The first Tiger black was Ozzie Virgil, a nondescript infielder who went to Detroit in 1958 after several years in the Giants' system. But the enlightened Red Sox managed to hold out until the sixties. Then they brought up Pumpsie Green, whose principal claim to fame was his magnificent nickname.

Yawkey, Cronin, and Murphy may not have been the stumbling blocks, but whoever it was signed only those black ballplayers who seemed to have little chance of making it to the majors. In 1955, I met two young blacks at

Ocala, Florida, where for years the Red Sox had a training
camp for their low minor-leaguers. Neither of that pair got
very far. Prior to that, the club didn't even have a token
black in their farm system.

Nor did they feel forced to find one even when the
Braves brought up Sam Jethroe before the club moved to
Milwaukee. Jethroe was an outfielder of doubtful talents,
although he was very fast and a pretty good hitter. Boston
fans remember him as perhaps the only man ever to be hit
on the head by a fly ball, in a pre-season city series game
against the Red Sox. Although he didn't leave much of a
dent in the record books, he was in the majors for some
years. The Braves had at least one black scout before they
left Boston and had already purchased Henry Aaron when
they shifted the franchise.

The first direct indication I had that some Red Sox people were against having a black player was one time in the
fifties, when Mike Higgins, then the manager, told me,
"There'll be no niggers on this ball club as long as I have
anything to say about it."

But Higgins, a Texan, was manager when Pumpsie
Green first went to spring training at Scottsdale. Although
he showed no signs of prejudice then, Higgins put the club
in an embarrassing position by taking Green along when
the team broke camp to barnstorm north, then sending him
to the minors along the way. This caused such a fuss among
civil-rights groups in Boston that Dick O'Connell had to
try to mollify them. Because he was in Boston while Higgins was traveling with the team, O'Connell took the rap
for Higgins's action. Taken by surprise when Green was
sent down, O'Connell had the unenviable job of trying to

explain what was as baffling to him as to everyone else. Since he was the only official handy, the civil rights people blamed him.

There would have been no problem if Higgins had released Green before leaving Scottsdale. Then it would have been obvious, even to those most interested in seeing a black player in a Red Sox uniform, that like any other rookie in a similar situation, Green wasn't ready for the majors. By waiting until the club left training camp before letting Green go, Higgins seemed to have given the young Negro false hopes, which made the disappointment of going to the minors even keener.

If they had chosen to, the Red Sox might have broken baseball's color line before the Dodgers did, and with a Hall of Fame star. Wendell Smith, a television news announcer in Chicago before his death, had been fighting the color line for years as sports editor of a Negro newspaper in Pittsburgh. Because of a quirk in Boston's Sunday baseball law, he saw a chance to force one of the Boston clubs to give black ballplayers a tryout in the spring of 1945.

At the time, although Boston had had Sunday baseball for some years, the law Smith found was that it had to be voted on unanimously for renewal every year by the Boston City Council. One of the council members, Isadore H. Y. Muchnick, represented Roxbury, originally a Jewish stronghold but rapidly becoming predominantly black. Smith suggested to Muchnick that he could insure a big black vote in his district by withholding his vote for Sunday baseball until one of the two ball clubs tried out a few black players. Since the Red Sox were the more popular team, Muchnick put the pressure on them, and they had no choice but to agree.

Smith brought three black players to Fenway Park for the tryout. They were Jackie Robinson, Sam Jethroe, and Emory Wright, all professionals in the Negro leagues. Jethroe and Wright failed to make much of an impression, but Robinson was fantastic. At the plate, he peppered the Wall with line drives and hit several over it. He showed a great arm and was all over the infield gobbling up ground balls and pop flies.

The tryout was supervised by the late Hugh Duffy, whose .438 batting average in 1894 as a member of the old Boston Red Stockings still stands as an all-time major-league record. He said later he had never seen such a magnificent prospect as Robinson. But Duffy was an old man with no real influence. Besides, in his capacity as director of tryouts for young unknowns he had no authority to make overtures toward signing a black star, which was then unheard of in baseball. And there was no hope of the tryouts getting much publicity even if the club released any, because that happened to be the day President Franklin D. Roosevelt died.

Smith took the players right from Boston to New York, where he contacted Branch Rickey, then president of the Brooklyn Dodgers. Rickey signed Robinson to the first contract ever given a black ballplayer in organized baseball.

There was a weird story, which I have never been able to check but which always sounded reasonable to me, that the Red Sox had a crack at Willie Mays before the Giants did. As a seventeen-year-old, Mays played for the Birmingham Black Barons, a Negro league team that had an agreement with the Birmingham Barons of the Southern Association to use the Barons' ball park when they were out of town. In return, the Barons had first refusal on any of the Black Barons' players.

That year the Red Sox had a working agreement with the Barons as Boston's Class Double A farm club. The Barons tipped the Red Sox on Mays, and they sent Larry Woodall, like Higgins a Texan, to Birmingham to look at him. It rained all the time Woodall was there. Without ever watching Mays play, Woodall gave the front office a more accurate report on the weather than on Mays and, as I heard the story, when he came home he still hadn't seen Mays in action. Everyone I asked around Fenway Park denied that this happened. But I would have denied it, too, if I had let a Willie Mays slip away right from under my nose. Imagine what the Red Sox might have done to the American League with Jackie Robinson and Willie Mays joining Ted Williams at Fenway Park!

One reason the Red Sox might not have been in a hurry to sign black ballplayers just after World War II was that they then had such a powerful team of white players. It was shortsighted of them not to look to an uncertain future, for the Williamses and Dom DiMaggios and Stephenses and Peskys and Doerrs certainly wouldn't last forever. Someone in authority obviously felt no pressure to sign Negroes. Only when the Tigers obtained Virgil did the Red Sox feel the pressure to bring a black player into the fold.

That Pumpsie Green was the man to break their color line could only have happened because of pressure. Red Sox brass had always said they would sign a black ballplayer when they found a good one, but at best Green was a fringe player, a utility infielder who couldn't even stick with the Mets when they were still baseball's most consistent and illustrious losers.

As it turned out, Green lasted longer with the Red Sox than a white player of his limited ability would have. A friendly, easy-going man, he was popular with players and press, and some of his adventures with the equally easy-going Gene Conley, a six-foot-eight white pitcher were truly hilarious. On the road, Conley and Green were inseparable. One reason they got along so well was their shared taste for beer. One hot day the Red Sox, after a series in New York against the Yankees, were on the team bus going to the airport, headed for Washington for a night game. They got stuck in traffic on the Triborough Bridge around noon. It was a stiflingly hot day, and the air-conditioning in the bus had broken down.

Finally, Conley started down the aisle, saying to nobody in particular, "I have to go to the bathroom."

"So do I," said Green, following him.

Just what happened then is not certain, except that both players assured the traveling secretary they would be at the airport in time to fly to Washington. They never made it. Instead, after apparently stopping at several spots, they ended up in an oasis on Lexington Avenue, where they basked in the air-conditioned cool and continued what apparently was a beer-drinking safari of monumental proportions.

By that time, a story that they had failed to show up for the Washington game had already broken in the newspapers. Suddenly, halfway through the night, Conley said,

"Let's go to Israel and teach baseball. Those poor people there don't know a thing about it."

"I think we should go to Washington," Green said.

"Look," said Conley, "I've got a thousand bucks in my pocket, so don't worry about the expense. We'll go to Israel, hire one of those two-humped camels, buy a couple of six-packs and go out into the desert and drink them."

"I don't know about you," Green said, "but I'm going to Washington."

"You know what I'll do if you don't go to Israel with me?" Conley said.

"What?"

"I'll drink your six-pack."

"Geno," said Green, "we're in enough trouble already. Forget Israel and come to Washington with me."

Green, who got more publicity out of that caper than he ever had out of baseball, wisely left the Lexington Avenue emporium and flew to Washington. Conley actually bought a ticket for Israel but couldn't get through customs because he had no passport. Eventually, he found his way to Washington, too, arriving there the day after Green. Pumpsie's defection did not impair their relationship, and they remained buddies as long as both were with the Red Sox.

Conley, who still lives in the Boston area, remembers Green with affection. In telling about the Israel adventure recently, he said, "Y'know, Pumpsie got scared when the story broke. When we saw it in the New York papers that night, he switched to milk. I guess that's why he wouldn't go to Israel with me. By the time I suggested it, he was too sober."

Unfortunately, the Green-Conley tieup was one of the

few interracial friendships on the Red Sox. Mostly there was little communication between blacks and whites, until the 1967 club worked together to win the pennant.

As I have previously indicated, the real problem was not at the top, but in the middle and lower echelons of the scouting system. In the mid-fifties, Yawkey told Neil Mahoney, who became the farm director in 1960, to find some black ballplayers of quality.

"I wish I could," Mahoney said. "But I'm in New England most of the time and we just don't have many here."

Yawkey also put pressure on John Murphy, who did send men out to look at black players. But they always came back with unfavorable or lukewarm reports. Murphy was responsible for a glaring omission in the farm system by not appointing a black scout or at least someone in a position to scout more blacks. He used too many of the old-time scouts to check on the few black ballplayers the Red Sox were tipped off about. It was these men, really, the older scouts, who can be blamed for the club's failure to get a top black player when plenty of good ones were available.

A typical example was a man Murphy used as a super-scout to make final checks on promising players. A local Red Sox scout in the southwest phoned in one day with word that a Negro baseball tournament was to be played the following week about a hundred miles from his base.

"I understand some of these boys are outstanding," he said. "And I'd like authority to sign a few."

He was told the club would send someone to go to the tournament with him, and the day before it began, Murphy's man appeared.

"How long is this nigger tournament going to last?" he demanded.

"Three days," the local scout said.

"Three days? I'm not hanging around here three days to watch a bunch of black kids. We'll go down tomorrow, hang around a few hours, and come back."

"That's no way to handle this," the local man said. "I know of two or three kids down there who can go all the way. And pretty nearly every team in the majors will have scouts there. We ought to go today, so we can see the first game in the morning."

"I'm playing golf today," the man from Boston retorted. "We'll go tomorrow."

The next day was a scorcher. The "superscout" slept late, then reluctantly started out just before noon. An hour later, still about thirty miles from their destination, he said, "Turn around and go back. I'm not going to sit through this thing."

The report he brought back to Boston was negative on all counts. He said, truthfully, that he hadn't seen one boy in the tournament worth signing.

"If I remember correctly, about a dozen of those kids were signed by other clubs," the southwestern scout told me later. "And half of them got up to the majors."

The first black prospect of real major-league potential to reach the Red Sox was Earl Wilson, the pitcher. A big, strong right-hander with a blazing fast ball, he pitched a no-hitter against the Angels in 1962. Traded to Detroit four years later, he won twenty-two games for the Tigers in 1967, then faded, finally retiring from baseball in 1970 after nine years in the majors. Wilson was a leader among the black Red Sox players. A Californian, he was signed by Joe Stephenson, a white scout.

When Neil Mahoney became farm director in 1960, one of his first moves was to sign Pedro Vazquez, a white Puerto Rican, to scout the Caribbean. Vazquez, who once announced big-league games in Spanish for Latin-American listeners, did a remarkable job. Some of the black Red Sox rookies now coming into the majors—men like Juan Beniquez, Ben Oglivie, and Rogelio Moret—were signed by Vazquez. After his death, Mahoney hired Felix Maldonado, also white and Puerto Rican, to handle the Caribbean area. It's hard to believe, in view of the rich lode of black ballplayers constantly coming up to the majors from Latin America, but the Red Sox never had a Caribbean scout before Vazquez.

Mahoney has since hired several black scouts, the most effective of whom has been Ed Scott, who works out of Mobile with Milt Bolling, a former infielder and front office executive. The two team up on occasion, with Bolling talking to white prospects, Scott to blacks, and each checking on the other's prospects. It was Ed Scott who signed George Scott (no relation), the next good black player to reach the Red Sox after Wilson. George, in the majors since 1966, was one of the men sent to Milwaukee in a ten-player swap right after the 1971 season ended.

Far and away the best black ballplayer Boston has ever had was Reggie Smith, a switch-hitting outfielder who at this writing has twice hit home runs from both sides of the plate in the same game. The Red Sox paid $8000 when they drafted him from the Minnesota Twins, who left him unprotected in 1963. A durable athlete who averages over

150 games a season, Smith, up to 1972, had twice batted over .300 and twice led the American League in doubles. He is also a superb fielder.

Smith and Carl Yastrzemski have been close friends for years, the best black-white relationship since Green and Conley. While each rooms alone on the road, they are inseparable and rarely miss eating together when traveling with the ball club.

Joe Foy, who faltered badly after a good season in 1967, was another black to come up through the Red Sox farm system, after being drafted from Washington. He had great potential and seemed headed for stardom, but his remarkable appetite for fattening foods did him in. He couldn't keep his weight within reasonable limits and faded out of the big leagues after only a few years.

After Foy was traded to Kansas City, the Red Sox had only two blacks (Smith and Scott) for nearly one full season. But there is now absolutely no reluctance anywhere in the organization to sign black ballplayers. Neil Mahoney knew who was most responsible for the long-term attempts to keep the team lily white, and he got rid of those men as soon as he could. But he didn't succeed in cleaning them all out until after Mike Higgins was fired as general manager in 1965.

The Red Sox haven't taken a bum rap on dragging their feet, but Tom Yawkey certainly has. The worst he was guilty of was too much trust in his department heads and the men under them. Murphy must have known who in the farm system was prejudiced against blacks and who wasn't. To send scouts who repeatedly showed their prejudice out to check on black prospects was bad enough. To trust their judgment and believe their scouting reports was insane.

And, while I'm sure he had no prejudices either, I think the same goes for Joe Cronin.

This is why I'm inclined to believe the Willie Mays story. Larry Woodall was the last man to send to Birmingham to check on Mays. Woodall resented having to hang around town waiting for the rain to stop, because he was being inconvenienced by a black. And in the years just before Mays was snapped up by the Giants, few Texans were liberal enough to hang around a southern city for days waiting to watch a seventeen-year-old black boy play ball.

If there ever were any doubts in my mind about Yawkey's feelings, they were dispelled the day the Red Sox clinched the 1967 pennant. There were six blacks on that team: Elston Howard, John Wyatt, Joe Foy, George Scott, Reggie Smith, and Jose Tartabull. Yawkey could have settled for a handshake and a pat on the back in the locker room for everyone on the club. But Yawkey threw a party for the whole team and their wives in his private suite at Fenway Park, and was equally gracious to everyone.

Yet their reluctance to sign black ballplayers when they could have had good ones, their pokiness in bringing up the first one, their selection of a man of Pumpsie Green's limited talents to break the race barrier, and their treatment of him the year he first reported to them in spring training, all added up to a serious, long-term fault in the Red Sox organization.

Black stars were helping other big-league teams win pennants long before the Red Sox took Green to Boston for the first time. And that was one of the things most seriously wrong with the ball club. It was another case of Tom Yawkey being done dirt by the people he trusted most.

CHAPTER 9

Down on the Farm

Branch Rickey devised the farm system in the late twenties when he ran the St. Louis Cardinals. One of the first major-league teams to follow his example were the Red Sox. A few years after Yawkey bought the ball club, Eddie Collins told him he couldn't go on buying established stars forever. The club, Collins insisted, had to start a farm system in which they could develop their own ballplayers.

Yawkey agreed, and a huge bundle of cash was set aside for the purpose. The first farm director was Billy Evans, a former major-league umpire with a reputation for spotting promising young players. Like Collins, he was enthusiastic about Rickey's idea and interested in building a powerful farm organization.

Evans wasn't with the ball club long enough to see any of his kids move up to Boston, because he accepted an offer to become general manager of the Cleveland Indians. He was succeeded by Herb Pennock, but Pennock died unexpectedly soon after he got the job. After World War II, which set back all the farm systems, the Red Sox made George Toporcer their farm director.

Toporcer did some organizing, but his failing eyesight (he later became blind) made it impossible for him to continue on the job. One interesting incident occurred while Toporcer was in charge. In those days, he traveled to look at hot prospects, but let his area scouts sign young players who appeared run-of-the-mill.

One day he had a report from his New York City scout on a high school third baseman in Manhattan.

"He'll never make it to the majors," the report said, "but we can use him in the farm system."

When Toporcer asked how big a bonus the boy wanted, he was told the kid would play for nothing—all he wanted was a chance.

"Give him five hundred dollars," Toporcer said.

Which was how Boston got Frank Malzone. He became one of the best all-around ballplayers they ever had, a fine hitter, and one of the top ten fielding third basemen in modern American League history. He now scouts the two major leagues for the Red Sox and helps advise them on deals with other clubs. After the 1967 World Series, Manager Dick Williams said Malzone's report on the Cardinals helped them force the far superior St. Louis club to the Series limit of seven games.

John Murphy followed Toporcer. He held the job about ten years, moving into it right from the dugout. Murphy seemed to have no particular qualifications except his close friendship with Joe Cronin. During his years in the front office, Murphy did nothing sensational. However, when he later joined the newly formed New York Mets, first as special assistant to the general manager and then as GM himself, he helped build the club from a hopeless tail-ender to the 1969 world champions.

He couldn't have made many mistakes in New York because he left most of them in Boston. He was not the only one to blame, but since it was his farm system for a decade, he had to be held partly responsible for the gradual collapse of the Red Sox. They didn't end their long downhill slide until their ninth-place finishes in 1965 and 1966, long after Murphy left them.

Despite his inadequacies, Murphy did build a farm system of formidable proportions. At the time he left, the Red Sox had something like fifty scouts, about half of whom were practically family retainers. And at one point the Red Sox owned or had working agreements with twelve minor-league teams, covering all classes from D to Triple A.

They picked up a tremendous amount of young talent before the high school and college draft went into effect in 1965. I was told by a number of farm directors and general managers of other big league teams that before 1965 the Red Sox, especially during the fifties, were in the bonus bidding battles for practically every outstanding white ballplayer who turned professional in that period. They obtained most of these boys simply by outbidding everyone else.

"I don't know what the hell happens to them," one executive said several years ago. "The pitchers come up with sore arms, the hitters get bad backs, and the fielders never improve. Time after time, the Red Sox beat everyone else in signing great-looking youngsters, but God only knows how they handle them once they have them."

His opinion was echoed by others in similar positions. Everyone in baseball except perhaps the Red Sox themselves knew there was something wrong. The kids had lots of natural ability, but most stumbled somewhere along the way. This was the case all through the fifties until Neil Mahoney, who succeeded Murphy in 1960, rebuilt the whole operation. Mahoney didn't have a really free hand until Higgins left in 1965, and was hobbled by the ineffiency of others in his first few years.

The problem really was inaction. The top Red Sox executives were unwilling to take chances. Until O'Connell became general manager, there hadn't been a major change in the overall operation of the ball club and its satellites since Eddie Collins's time. This included the farm system, which, although it grew, didn't really change.

Like too many other departments at Fenway Park, the farm system was an aristocracy of cronyism. The same men held the same jobs for years, whether they handled them properly or not. It didn't matter what a man did; the important thing was whom he knew, and how well. The whole system was built around old friendships and old associations. When a favored guy (witness Murphy) finished his playing career, he was assured of a job in the organization. If he couldn't be a coach with the big club, he might manage one of the minor-league clubs. If there weren't any openings, he could become a scout, or a job would be created for him. He could always become somebody's special assistant. That title covered a multitude of possibilities—and sins.

The farm system, cumbersome and antiquated, remained the same until Mahoney became its head. He did as much streamlining as he was permitted to, although not as much as he knew was necessary. After O'Connell became general manager in 1965, one of the first things Mahoney discussed with him was splitting up the duties at the top. Until then, the farm director was in charge of just about everything short of the big-league team.

This had several disadvantages. The most glaring was that the farm director, who had the last word in signing a ballplayer also assigned him his first minor-league team and decided how fast he would move up. The director often did this without seeing the player in action. He would say, "O.K., Joe Pitcher is a great prospect. We'll start him in Double A, put him into Triple A next year, then recommend that he go with the big club the year after."

It didn't matter if Joe Pitcher fell on his face in Double A or Triple A. His future had been mapped out by the farm director, who naturally would look very bad if Joe didn't make it to the Red Sox in three years.

And that was another problem. The farm director's philosophy was, "No matter what happens, *we can't look bad.* When we sign a great prospect, it's our ass, not his, if he fails. Therefore, make sure he doesn't fail."

This, of course, eliminated the human element almost entirely. If Joe Pitcher didn't turn out to be as good as he looked at his signing, he kept moving right up through the farm system anyhow. The farm director would report his "progress" to the general manager from time to time. Since the general manager didn't have time to see Joe Pitcher in action, he took the director's word for it.

So the farm director was judge and jury, defense and prosecution. This was one of the reasons Mahoney—who was well aware of the problem from his own experience within the system—and O'Connell agreed to split the job up. As it happened, Mahoney had a heart attack in 1965, brought on largely by the double load he was carrying. The job was just too big for one man.

But it was neither his age nor the heart attack that dictated the separation of powers. That had already been decided on. Mahoney became director of scouting and player procurement, and Ed Kenney, who had been his assistant, was made director of minor-league clubs. Thus, once a player was signed by Mahoney, his future was out of the director's hands. Kenney decided where the signee would start, and after that his progress up through the system depended simply on his performance. And neither Mahoney nor Kenney care whether *they* look bad or not. If a dark horse emerges from the pack of kids, he gets moved up as fast as a high bonus player who is making similar progress. Performance has become the key. Until Mahoney took over, performance was almost incidental.

One of the first problems O'Connell straightened out was the system of evaluating minor-league prospects.

"If you listened to our scouts," he told me, "you had nothing but hot shots. Obviously, a scout isn't going to put the slug on a man he has recommended; he wants to see that man move up as quickly as possible. But our people were praising their own men too lavishly. Every outfielder was another Ted Williams, every infielder another Brooks Robinson, every pitcher another Bob Feller."

The matter was complicated by the fact that the Boston press and the Red Sox scouts often met at spring training. When a ballplayer looked especially good there, some writer would usually find the scout who discovered him and ask what he thought. Naturally, he got the same answer every time: "Can't miss."

Then the writer would quote the scout, the other papers would pick it up, and the next thing the club knew they had a terrific prospect who couldn't possibly end up anywhere except in Boston.

This put pressure on everybody—the ballplayer, the manager, veteran ballplayers in the same position as the youngster, the front office, even the press. And when, as was usually the case, the young player in question turned out to be a dud or just not ready, the Boston fans would say, "How come?"

Obviously, nobody could supply the answer. The kid had looked great when spring training began, but most kids look great at that point. To begin with, many arrive at spring training fresh from a season of winter ball, so they are in better shape than the veterans, some of whom haven't touched a baseball since the end of the previous season. In the second place, they are full of energy, ambition, and confidence. And in the third, when spring training begins, the best pitchers in camp are the mechanical pitching machines. The human ones don't get around to pitching hard for some time.

Ring Lardner was the first to point out that great young prospects too often die on the vine when "the pitchers start curving them." When a seasoned major-league pitcher is ready, a green rookie reaches the moment of truth. If he passes that test, he begins to look like a big-league possibility.

The same thing is true, in reverse, of rookie pitchers.

Almost all pitchers have sore arms the first week of spring training—all but those who have been playing winter ball or have been working the kinks out of their arms at home. When Joe Pitcher, right out of Puerto Rico or Venezuela, where he's been playing ball all winter, faces Carl Ya-strzemski or Reggie Smith or Rico Petrocelli the first week of the training season, Joe Pitcher really does look like the second coming of Bob Feller. It's only if he can get these veteran hitters out in the last week of spring training that he's worth writing about.

Rogelio Moret, a Puerto Rican who came up to the Red Sox from the minors for the third time in 1973, was a case in point. After Moret won eleven games and lost seven for Pawtucket in the Eastern League in 1970, the Red Sox took him to Boston, where he won one game. A year later, after an 11–8 record at Louisville, the Triple A club, Moret came to Boston again. This time he had a 4–3 record.

When he looked good early in spring training in 1972, the press, which had observed him thoroughly, did just what the scouts used to do—tagged him as a "can't miss" prospect. Loaded with pressure, Moret didn't make it and went back to Louisville.

"We didn't know how great a pitcher we had in Moret until we saw it in the papers," O'Connell told me in 1972 at Winter Haven. "He's a good prospect. He might make it. We hope he does. But he hasn't developed into a real big-league pitcher yet. And building him up as such a hotshot doesn't help anyone. Hell, he's not even the best-looking rookie pitcher in camp right now."

John Curtis and Lynn McGlothen, both of whom developed so fast that they were in the regular Red Sox pitching rotation as rookies by June of 1972, were the best. They got good publicity in Winter Haven that spring, too, but not as much as Moret.

It has always been easy to blame the press for going overboard on kids. Perhaps, now that the scouts are more careful in evaluating youngsters, the writers are more at fault than anyone else in overpraising rookies, but they weren't always. When Red Sox scouts were trying to push the youngsters they signed, they used the press as one weapon to keep a favored boy with the big club. More often than not, it worked—at least for a while.

One of the biggest problems of the Red Sox farm system was—especially when the big team trained in Arizona —an insanely expensive geographical spread of spring training sites. The Red Sox were in Scottsdale, their Triple A team trained in Deland, Florida, and all the other minor leaguers trained in Ocala, Florida. At one point, when the Triple A boys played in Seattle, it cost more money to trot them around than the big leaguers.

This arrangement remained in effect through Bucky Harris's and Mike Higgins's tenures as GM. The Red Sox finally escaped from Arizona and opened their Winter Haven quarters in 1966. But even then, with all three groups in Florida, it was a nuisance shuttling coaches, special instructors, and players.

O'Connell wanted to get all the players into the same community, but not under one roof. Not only was it tough to keep moving everyone around, but both Ocala and Deland were well off the beaten spring training path. The clubs had trouble arranging games with other teams of their own caliber. While the big club could go anywhere in Florida to play exhibition games, it was hardly worth while to send the minor-league teams all over the state for competition.

Plans were made as far back as 1969 to have all the farm teams train in Winter Haven, but they couldn't be carried out until 1972, because of Winter Haven's lack of accommodations. O'Connell's reluctance to put everyone under the same roof was based on the possibilities of discontent in the lower echelons. The higher the class, the better the facilities. By 1973, the Red Sox were housed in one hotel, the Triple A Louisville Colonels in another, and the rest of the minor leaguers in a third. But they all practiced within a stone's throw of each other, since new diamonds were built adjacent to Chain O' Lakes Park, where the Red Sox work out and play their spring exhibition games and where their Florida State League team plays its regular season games.

With all the teams training in the same community, everyone gets the benefit of the best instruction in the system. Until 1972, the top instructors had to travel around, so that they were available only part of the time. For example, the Red Sox pitching coach (Lee Stange at this writing) was never able to help pitchers except in Winter Haven. His first obligation was to the Red Sox, of course, and he had his hands full with their rookies. But from 1972 on, he could be called on if necessary to help solve a difficult problem with a minor-league prospect.

Bill Slack, the chief minor-league pitching coach, no longer has to make the long rounds to different training camps. Neither does Gene Conley, his assistant (who never did make it to Israel, by the way). Nor Darrell Johnson, brought in as Red Sox pitching coach by Dick Williams in 1968. Johnson remained with the organization after Williams left, and now manages the top farm club at Pawtucket, R.I. When Eddie Kasko, who has done a solid job as manager, meets the inevitable fate of all major-league managers, Johnson is nearly certain to succeed him. In the meantime, besides managing Pawtucket, Johnson is available to help with pitching problems that come up anywhere in the organization.

Sam Mele, a traveling superscout, is also a sort of superinstructor in spring training. So is Frank Malzone, although Malzone concentrates most of his efforts on the big-league team. For example, when Rico Petrocelli was switched from shortstop to third base to make room for Luis Aparicio, who had been a major-league all-star shortstop for years, Malzone worked with Petrocelli. Although not yet as good a third baseman as he was a shortstop, Petrocelli has improved tremendously since the end of the 1970 season. Before Malzone is through with him, Petrocelli should be outstanding.

There was that serious breakdown in communications between the farm office and the brass during the years Bucky Harris was general manager. This was the reason the Red Sox lost Gene Mauch, whom they were grooming for manager of the big club. Both Cronin and Murphy promised him the job when it opened, and they really intended to follow through on it. But when Harris succeeded Cronin, he either didn't know or didn't care that Mauch was available, and without consulting Murphy, he reappointed Billy Jurges as manager for 1960. That triggered Mauch's acceptance of the Phillies' job.

There was also little communication between Higgins as general manager and Mahoney as farm director. Mahoney, who spent a good deal of time on the road looking at prospects, sent his reports to Higgins (with copies to Yawkey, as is the custom in all Red Sox departments). But Higgins rarely sought Mahoney's advice.

This communications gap has long since been closed by O'Connell and Mahoney, who have been friends for years as comparative underlings in the Red Sox system. They spent many hours discussing what should be done that wasn't, just as all minor employees do. Unlike most, these two were given the chance to put their theories into effect, with excellent results.

For example, when O'Connell was made general manager in September of 1965, Manager Billy Herman was just finishing the first year of the two-year contract Higgins had given him. With the team going nowhere, O'Connell's first inclination was to fire Herman. But this would mean paying him for the 1966 season while a manager of O'Connell's choosing ran the club from the bench.

"Keeping Herman was partly to give him a fair chance," O'Connell told me. "But that was only one of the factors. I knew Billy was a golf nut, but he had also been a great ballplayer, and I hoped that with a better young club, he'd pay more attention and generate more enthusiasm. If he did, he might lead the Red Sox up the ladder a little.

"I was wrong," he added. "Herman was no better in 1966 than in 1965. But what if I had fired him? How the hell did I know who might make a better manager for us? I wasn't a baseball man. My job had been to handle just about all phases of the club operation except the team. I wanted a good young executive with a solid baseball background to handle player personnel, including helping me pick a new manager if we had to. I wasn't afraid of the responsibility, but I simply didn't feel I was equipped to pick the right manager. And a month or so after I got the job was certainly not the time for me to fire the manager we had, especially since he had another year to go on his contract. That's why I spent so much time looking for an executive instead of a new manager in the months after the 1965 season ended."

When O'Connell chose Haywood Sullivan, then manager of Charley Finley's Kansas City A's, a good many New England fans thought he was crazy. Not that Sullivan was a total stranger to Boston sports followers. He was remembered as a promising young catcher whose career had been ruined by a back operation. Sullivan had once formed a battery with a delightfully screwball pitcher named Frank Sullivan. (When Curt Gowdy was the radio and television voice of the Red Sox, he once asked Frank Sullivan what sort of season he expected to have. "It will probably be my last," Sullivan replied. "I have the feeling I am nearing the climax of a mediocre career.")

Another thing Red Sox buffs knew was that when Frank Sullivan pitched and Haywood Sullivan caught, there wasn't a Catholic in the house. Sullivan is a good old Boston Irish Catholic name, yet here were two Boston ballplayers named Sullivan (not related, incidentally), and both were Protestants.

Haywood Sullivan had one other public distinction. He was the only manager Charley Finley ever had who left the job voluntarily. What the fans didn't know was that this huge young man (he stood six-four and was still in his mid-thirties) was one of baseball's most promising executives. A college graduate, a sharp observer of youthful talent, and with far more than the average dose of common sense, Haywood Sullivan was thoroughly qualified to handle the job O'Connell had hired him for.

Perhaps the best example of Sullivan's ability to judge baseball talent was the selection of Dick Williams as the 1967 manager. This was the result of perfect cooperation among the general manager, the player personnel director, and the farm system office. O'Connell needed no brain trust to fire Herman when the club was again resting comfortably in ninth place in the dying weeks of the 1966 season. But he relied heavily on Sullivan's judgment of whether to replace Herman from inside the system or go elsewhere for the new manager.

Dick Williams was the leading candidate from the beginning, so O'Connell had Sullivan virtually commuting between Boston and Toronto from about midseason on. Williams managed Toronto, the club's top farm before it was moved to Louisville. (It was shifted to Pawtucket in 1973.) Only after frequent conferences with Sullivan, Neil Mahoney, and Ed Kenney did O'Connell promote Williams to the Boston job.

The same type of cooperation among the general manager, the player personnel director, and the farm office resulted in the appointment of Eddie Kasko, who had been the Louisville manager, to succeed Williams. There are still frequent meetings between farm office and front office brass, covering all phases of the farm operation. In 1972, the Red Sox came up with some fine rookies, each of whom had been thoroughly discussed before being moved to the big club.

Contrast this type of organization with the days of the Red Sox dark ages, the early fifties to the mid-sixties. At one point during that time the farm office spent over half a million dollars in bonuses for catchers alone. One of the bonus catchers, Frank Isbell, never even showed up for spring training. He just took the money and ran. To my knowledge, the only ones who made a major-league dent were Haywood Sullivan and Gerry Zimmerman. Zimmerman, dropped after several years in the organization, made it to the Reds in 1961, then spent seven years with the Twins. Except for Sullivan, it was all money down the drain, and Sullivan today does much more for the Red Sox as an executive than he ever did as a player.

Yet, to do him justice, Cronin's orders to Murphy were hardly different from O'Connell's to Mahoney—just get good ballplayers, no matter where they play. The difference is that Cronin hardly knew one bonus baby from another, while O'Connell stays right on top of the situation.

When the Red Sox signed Carl Yastrzemski for $108,000 plus college tuition and a good minor-league salary in 1958, Cronin didn't even know Yastrzemski's dimensions. When Murphy introduced the five-eleven, 170-pound youngster to Cronin, the boss turned to Murphy and said, "He doesn't seem very big."

Since the high school and college draft, which began in 1965, the day of tremendous bonuses is just about over. Scouts can no longer sign any good prospect they find. All they can do is watch the kids and recommend how they should be ranked in the draft. This requires a different kind of scout than in the old bonus days. Then, rival scouts romanced young prospects, spending weeks, months, and sometimes years getting to know a boy and his parents. Except when the bonus was unusually big, the scout actually signed the player when he became eligible.

Now, the higher the draft choice, the higher the bonus. Every club wants to sign its number-one selection, especially if they are high in the order of choosing. As in other sports, the baseball draft is based on the order of finish the previous season, with the lowest team getting first choice, the next lowest second, and so on. Since the World Series winner gets the leavings, their first choice is actually twenty-fourth on the list. If he's an outstanding ballplayer, someone else will almost surely have picked him up by the time the champions get their turn. And they may not be so crazy about the man they can get that they will offer a lot for his signature. On the other hand, if he looks better to their scouts than to the scouts from other clubs, they might give him a pretty good bonus, particularly if he's in demand for another sport's draft.

In any event, the scout's judgment now is more important than his personal charm and the money behind him. That's why baseball scouting is an altogether different game from what it was before 1965. Most clubs, including the Red Sox, find it more expedient to have several scouts watch a boy in action from time to time than to assign one scout the full-time job.

"We still check the intangibles," Mahoney told me. "We still want to know what kind of boy he is, if he has a good reputation, is fundamentally decent and not a troublemaker. But there's no point in spending a lot of money working on a player who's likely to go to another team."

The streamlining and updating of the Red Sox farm system has eliminated another evil—blind adherence to old-fashioned theories. In the fifties, the farm system was as modern as the Floradora Girls. If a young pitcher wasn't big or if he lacked an overpowering fast ball, the hell with him. If a young pitcher *was* big, said the book, he could be taught to throw an overpowering fast ball, as well as a curve, a slider, or a change. But the fast ball came first. Nothing could get in the way of that.

With a Frank Baumann or a Maurice McDermott, that was fine. Baumann, according to Ed Kenney, who has worked in the farm office for many years, "was the fastest schoolboy pitcher I ever saw. I don't see how *any* high school boy could hit him. And McDermott was next."

Kenney also pointed out that while the old farm system may have had faults, it couldn't be held responsible for Baumann's troubles.

"This boy had one tremendous year in Triple A, then hurt his arm while he was in the service," Kenney said. "You couldn't blame the farm office for that."

True. Any more than you could blame the farm office because McDermott wouldn't take care of himself. But a typical case that you *could* blame on the farm office was Wilbur Wood's.

Wood grew up in the Boston suburb of Belmont, where he was an outstanding pitcher. A skinny six-foot southpaw, he starred at Belmont High School, and in 1960, when he graduated, the Red Sox signed him for a $30,000 bonus. He had a pretty good fast ball, a pretty good curve, and remarkable control, which is most unusual for an eighteen-year-old left-hander.

He also had a knuckler, an off-speed pitch he had been using since junior high school. This is a very tricky pitch which, if mastered, is an automatic ticket to long-term big-league success, because it is effective and puts no strain on the arm. Despite his tender years when he signed the contract, Wood was quite aware of this point. He hadn't perfected the pitch, but he was sure he could if given proper instruction.

But down on the Red Sox farm, the coaches wouldn't let Wood use it. (They didn't have anybody who could throw it, let alone teach someone else to throw it.) They told Wood to concentrate on his fast ball and his curve. He was big enough to throw a good fast ball and smart enough to improve his curve. But the important thing, according to the book, was the fast ball, and nobody went more by the book than the Red Sox. Take a big strong boy. Make him throw more fast balls than anything else. Feed him well and be sure he exercises, so the food will become muscle, not fat. In due time, with his fast ball, he will be a winner. Didn't Walter Johnson prove it? And Bob Feller? And Lefty Grove?

So Wilbur Wood put his knuckler on the shelf. His fast ball was fast enough for the minors, but not quite fast enough for the majors. His curve ball broke well enough for the minors, but not quite enough for the majors. His control continued to be outstanding. The result was predictable to a casual observer, if not to Wood's trained teachers in the farm system. He became a great minor-league pitcher and a pigeon in the majors. The Red Sox brought him to Boston three times. They then had to let him go, because by baseball law one club cannot send a man to the minors more than three times. The Pirates picked Wood up, but he didn't make it with them either. In 1967, at the age of twenty-six, he landed with the White Sox.

There, with the ageless Hoyt Wilhelm to help him, Wood resurrected the knuckler which the Red Sox wouldn't let him throw and the Pirates didn't know he had. At this writing Wood, who turned thirty-one in October of 1972, relying almost exclusively on his knuckler, is one of baseball's best pitchers. Every time he beats the Red Sox, New England fans cry a lot and die a little.

The farm system was not a total loss under John Murphy. A few good ballplayers made it to the majors. But, as in Wood's case, it was like running an obstacle course. They went all the way in spite of their handling, not because of it. And there were some outstanding men in the farm system faculty, notably Eddie Popowski, a Red Sox coach since 1967.

The men who did best were those who went through the system the fastest, like Carl Yastrzemski. He spent only two years in the minors before arriving in Boston to stay in 1961. There wasn't time to louse him up. But Yastrzemski was one of those rare superstars who couldn't have been ruined by anyone.

Today, the Red Sox farm system is a good one. But it wasn't always. Before Neil Mahoney and Dick O'Connell had any authority, it was one of the most expensive and yet one of the poorest in organized baseball.

CHAPTER 10

A Trade or Two

There is no easier or more infuriating pastime in baseball than second-guessing trades. No matter how lousy a ballplayer may be, he will have a good day now and then, so whenever a traded player looks good, the deal looks bad for the team that traded him. This happens to all clubs, but nobody keeps a closer eye on traded players than those who follow the fortunes of the Red Sox.

In common with every other team in the major leagues, they have made their share of mistakes. This includes the present organization headed by Dick O'Connell, as well as past hierarchies. Any trade can backfire. Any player can come back to haunt the club that dumped him. And by his performance, any player can brand a team that gets rid of him as a collection of dopes who should have known better than to send him down the river.

For years New England fans have pointed with fiendish delight to successful players on other clubs who once belonged to the Red Sox. A classic case is Jim Fregosi, for many years a standout with the California Angels, who now stars for the Mets when he is healthy. Fregosi started in the Red Sox organization, but was left unprotected in the expansion draft of 1960. The Angels picked him up, and he went on to fame and fortune on the west coast.

But the Red Sox didn't make the worst trade in baseball history. That honor belongs to the Cincinnati Reds, who sent the peerless Frank Robinson to the Baltimore Orioles for Milt Pappas after the 1965 season. Robinson proceeded to spark the Orioles to four pennants in six years, while Pappas didn't spark anything, although he pitched a no-hitter for the Cubs in 1972. Even at the height of their frequent periods of stupidity, the Red Sox never made a deal that bad.

Today, teams try to make their most important trades when interleague deals are permitted, roughly between the end of the regular season and the middle of December. It's pretty safe to trade even an outstanding star to the other league because the chances of his hurting his old ball club are minimal. There's always a possibility that he will play against them in a World Series, but that's rare.

To analyze all the deals Boston has made down through the years would be pointless. Single man-for-man trades aren't important unless one or both players are stars. Deals involving second-line or fringe players seldom have significance either. This is almost always garbage for garbage, with nobody caring one way or the other and neither team either benefiting or getting burnt.

But some deals are worth looking back on, because they show both the good and bad sides of the Red Sox as flesh peddlers. In the early days of the Yawkey regime, the Red Sox were the most active team in baseball, but they weren't trading then. They were buying. It was at the height of the Great Depression, and Tom Yawkey was one of the few owners with money to spare. At that time, an indigent club could stay alive only by selling off its outstanding players. Today it's impossible to buy a ranking star for mere cash because no team who has such talent is that broke. And big-league teams always want to improve their personnel, which they can't do by accepting just money for an established standout.

Yawkey nearly bought a pennant or two in the thirties. The only reason he failed was that his pitchers and hitters never seemed to click at the same time. And at best, the Red Sox fielding was never quite good enough to give the club the kind of defense a championship team must have.

But the millions Yawkey spent in those days weren't wasted. He transformed a sick franchise into one of the healthiest and best in baseball. He did it with money, because you could do that at the time. And anything that could be done with money the Red Sox did.

Even following World War II, after the Red Sox won the 1946 pennant, they could still buy good ballplayers. Witness the two gigantic deals with the St. Louis Browns after Boston's pitching staff collapsed with sore arms in 1947. Although the deals involved a lot of men, they were fundamentally money deals, with heavy cash going from Boston to St. Louis, and outstanding talent coming the other way.

Those deals, in which Boston got Junior Stephens, Jack Kramer, Ellis Kinder, and Billy Hitchcock, were the last in which the Red Sox were able to buy stars for cash plus flocks of dispensable men. From then on, their trades were riskier and riskier. Today, every trade is a risk. When a club has a great ballplayer, it will think many times before dealing him off for anyone else.

The winter between 1971 and 1972, when stars like Frank Robinson, Dick Allen, Alex Johnson, Lee May, Joe Morgan, Jim Fregosi, Ken Holtzman, Gaylord Perry, Rick Monday, and Sam McDowell all changed uniforms, was one of the most active off-seasons the big leagues have ever known. But everyone on that list except Johnson, May, and Morgan changed leagues. Robinson went from the Orioles to the Dodgers, Allen from the Dodgers to the White Sox, Fregosi from the Angels to the Mets, Holtzman from the Cubs to the A's for Monday, who went the other way, and McDowell from the Indians to the Giants for Perry, who also went the other way.

Boston also made a gigantic deal during that same off-season. On October 11, 1971, they sent Ken Brett, Jim Lonborg, Don Pavletich, Joe Lahoud, George Scott, and Billy Conigliaro to Milwaukee for Marty Pattin, Tommy Harper, Lew Krausse, and Pat Skrable. All of New England was up in arms over that one. To the average observer, it looked like a steal for the Brewers.

But Brett, a very promising young southpaw, had never produced for the Red Sox. Lonborg, the ace in the successful 1967 pennant drive, was never the same after his ski accident in December of that year. Pavletich and Lahoud were fringe ballplayers. Scott, a great fielder, had never developed into the slugger he should have become. And Billy Conigliaro, a good hitter and fair outfielder, was a problem child who had lost his taste for baseball completely after the Red Sox had traded his brother, Tony, to California the year before.

Yet in the early stages of the 1972 season, the trade looked very bad from Boston's point of view. Lonborg, as he had since his accident, pitched a few very good games for Milwaukee. So did Brett. Scott and Conigliaro hit well. In the meantime, Pattin lost his first six starts, Krausse did only a fair relief job, and Skrable went to the minors. Only Harper, the regular center fielder from the start, really stood up.

Then everything began falling into place. Pattin regained his pitching equilibrium and won a string of victories, including a one-hitter that just missed being a no-hitter. With Sonny Siebert having difficulty getting started and Ray Culp on the injured list, Pattin was the club's stopper by midseason. Harper continued to play well, and Krausse came up with some good relief jobs.

In the meantime, only Scott did consistently well in Milwaukee. Lahoud and Pavletich contributed little, while Lonborg and Brett were in and out. And when Conigliaro, as unpredictable as his brother but not half the ballplayer, retired in July, the Red Sox front office looked temporarily clairvoyant. Even the wolves who had screeched over the trade at the time quieted down.

The same thing had happened exactly a year before, on October 11, 1970, when the Red Sox traded Tony Conigliaro, catcher Gerry Moses, and pitcher Ray Jarvis to California for pitcher Ken Tatum, outfielder Jarvis Tatum, and Doug Griffin, a minor-league infielder nobody had ever heard of.

The fans and the press raised a terrible stink. The elder Conigliaro, after a stellar beginning (he was the first major leaguer to hit over 100 homers in his first three seasons), had apparently been knocked out of baseball for good when hit in the face by a pitched ball in 1967. After several days on the brink of death, he recovered, but one eye was so badly affected that ophthalmologists said he would never play again.

After a season and a half on the shelf, Conigliaro made a remarkable comeback. That, plus the fact that he was a local boy, gave him tremendous stature in Boston. But despite the comeback the Red Sox felt they had one too many Conigliaros on the club. Since Billy was younger, healthier, and a promising long-ball hitter, they decided to trade Tony. Close observers (the press) openly wondered if Dick O'Connell had lost his marbles. How could he deal off an apparently healthy Tony Conigliaro, the best-looking kid catcher they had, and a young pitcher for two Tatums (unrelated) and a guy named Griffin?

O'Connell himself provided the answer, but only when asked.

"Wait until you see the guy named Griffin," he said. "At Hawaii last year [1970] he was the best second baseman in the minors. And Ken Tatum is a good relief pitcher."

That deal turned out as well as the Milwaukee trade a year later. Griffin, Boston's regular second baseman ever since, did indeed turn out to be the big man in the trade. Although he hardly killed the customers, Ken Tatum didn't do badly in relief. The other Tatum was never a factor.

But look what happened to the men the Red Sox gave up. Tony Conigliaro's eye suddenly deteriorated, and he had to quit in midseason of 1971. Moses, never a ball of fire in Boston, was no better at California and went to Cleveland in the same deal with Alex Johnson. And Ray Jarvis slipped back into the minor leagues.

All of which proves that a deal never can be judged with much accuracy at the time it is made. O'Connell was neither clairvoyant nor a genius. He was very lucky in both the big trades.

He had no way of knowing that both the Conigliaros would be out of baseball within a year after they left Boston. (Billy returned in 1973 when the Angels traded him to the A's.) He took a chance on Griffin. Although reports on him were glowing, backed up by Haywood Sullivan's own observations of the kid, there was no guarantee he would make it in the majors. There never is with a rookie.

Perhaps the biggest gamble of all was letting Moses go. After reportedly collecting a bonus of $75,000 for signing, he had moved up through the farm system. Although no barn-burner, he looked reasonably good once he got into a Red Sox uniform. He could always hit, but he never developed into a good receiver. When the Red Sox let him go they left themselves without an experienced catcher. They had to trade with the White Sox for Duane Josephson, while still relying heavily on the rookie crop.

In that respect, they were either lucky or good. Bob Montgomery was passable. And by 1972, rookie Pudge Fisk was tremendous, hitting close to .300 and looking like a real major leaguer behind the plate. He made the American League All-Star team.

In 1969, the Red Sox made a deal so unpopular that the telephone operators were blinded by the red lights on the Fenway Park switchboard. Ten days after the season started, they traded Ken (Hawk) Harrelson and pitchers Dick Ellsworth and Juan Pizarro to Cleveland for Sonny Siebert, Vicente Romo, and catcher Joe Azcue. Harrelson was the reason for all the squawking. A Boston favorite as a ballplayer and as delightful a screwball as Frank Sullivan, he was a passable fielder and a great Fenway Park hitter. He had the range of the left field fence and had led the American League in runs batted in the year before.

If Siebert hadn't turned out unusually well (he had three winning seasons in a row and with Ray Culp gave the pitching staff a good one-two punch during that period), the trade probably wouldn't have been a particularly good one. Azcue quit because Dick Williams let him simmer on the bench for two weeks (some said *that* was what really cost Williams his job, although it wasn't). Romo pitched well at times, but couldn't be depended on and eventually was traded to the White Sox.

But in the long run the Indians got nothing out of the deal. All three of the men they picked up are now out of the majors. Ellsworth and Pizarro were near the end of the trail anyhow, and Harrelson retired in midseason of 1971 to try his hand on the professional golf circuit.

Of course, not all the trades made by the O'Connell organization have been complete successes from the club's viewpoint. For some reason, only three men from the pennant-winning 1967 team were left six years later. Since that was supposed to be the beginning of a Red Sox dynasty (Yastrzemski, the oldest regular, was twenty-eight and most of the others were twenty-five or under), it's amazing how quickly the team broke up. Only Yastrzemski, Reggie Smith, and Rico Petrocelli were left by 1973.

The last to go, Sparky Lyle, was traded to the Yankees for Danny Cater just after the 1972 opener. Lyle turned out to be the hottest reliever in the league, while Cater, although he finally began to hit near midseason, still hadn't proved he was a better man to have on the premises than Lyle.

As O'Connell himself said, the Red Sox had to weaken themselves in one place to shore up another. They needed good pitching behind Lonborg, so they obtained Culp and Ellsworth even before his midwinter skiing mishap. Until Fisk proved himself in 1972, they were always in trouble behind the plate. Even the 1967 club was weak there until Elston Howard came along, but Howard was only a stop-gap catcher. At thirty-eight, he was nearly through. He retired in 1968 to become a Yankee coach.

Looked at objectively, the 1967 club was loaded with weaknesses. The catching was vulnerable and the pitching spotty. The drop between Jim Lonborg, the ace of the staff, and the number-two pitcher, Jose Santiago, was something like ten games. Both Santiago and Gary Bell had their last good year in 1967. Bell, who came from Cleveland early in the season in a swap for Tony Horton, was nearly through then. Santiago, who might have had a few good years left, came up with a sore arm. The only other pitcher from the 1967 staff who ever really helped the ball club again was Lyle. He was an outstanding reliever in Boston for the next four years and perhaps should have been kept, for left-handed firemen of his caliber don't grow on trees.

George Scott, the first baseman, also had his last great season in 1967. Second baseman Mike Andrews was a good ballplayer who probably would still be in Boston if the Red Sox hadn't picked up Doug Griffin, who was better. Rico Petrocelli was a good shortstop, but eventually was needed worse at third. Joe Foy, the third baseman, was no better than passable there.

The outfield of Yastrzemski in left, Reggie Smith in center, and Tony Conigliaro in right was the best in baseball until Conigliaro was hurt. After that, right field was a problem until the Red Sox obtained Harper. He could play center and enable Smith to move over to right. Today, with Yastrzemski in left, Harper in center, and Smith in right, the outfield is still one of the best in the business, but Yastrzemski has become a first baseman.

If the 1967 team was that shaky, how did it win the pennant? The two most positive answers are Yastrzemski and Dick Williams. Few men ever dominated baseball as Yastrzemski did in 1967. He not only won the Triple Crown, but was the inspirational leader of a real team of destiny. No matter how hopeless the game or how little time was left, Yaz was always there to save the situation. Time after time he got key hits, many of them home runs, in clutches. Of course, everyone did his share, and other players were always picking up the slack. But Yaz delivered most often.

Williams took a ninth-place club, which never had much reason to do better, and made it into a champion. Yastrzemski provided the thrills and the inspiration, but Williams was the man who detonated the explosion. The ballplayers didn't like him personally, but as he said, he wasn't trying to win a popularity contest. He didn't care whether anybody liked him as long as they played ball for him. And that they did, adding a glittering page to the folklore of Fenway.

From a negative point of view, a principal factor in the Red Sox pennant was the collapse of the Baltimore pitching staff. The Orioles had won the pennant and World Series the year before. But in 1967 they were like the 1947 Red Sox: the pitchers came down with an epidemic of sore arms. That, plus a crippling injury suffered by Frank Robinson, dropped the Orioles out of the race early, and they finished sixth. In the resulting scramble, during which it was anybody's pennant, Williams and Yastrzemski made the difference.

Nobody knew all the weaknesses as well as Dick Williams, Dick O'Connell, and Haywood Sullivan. The pitching was weak, so they traded for Ellsworth and Culp. Ellsworth didn't do much, but Culp was a real find. If Lonborg hadn't found skiing for pleasure more important than pitching for money, the Red Sox would have been pennant contenders in 1968 and might even have won despite their weaknesses. But without Lonborg they were dead. They missed him more than they missed Tony Conigliaro.

Their fundamental weaknesses brought about other weaknesses through trades. Until Lonborg was hurt, they could trade from strength. With Lonborg out, they needed pitching help, and in order to get it they had to trade from weakness. Any deal they made might solve one problem but create another.

Foy's failure complicated matters, as did George Scott's collapse at the plate. At least Scott's fielding continued at the highest level of efficiency, and he could play either first base or third. But, as O'Connell later explained, "We had to give to get."

When they traded Harrelson in early 1969, they weakened themselves at the plate to beef up the battery. Azcue was a better catcher than anyone the Red Sox had. Siebert was a solid pitcher, and Romo a good reliever. Dick Williams's failure to use Azcue and Azcue's resultant refusal to stay with the club proved, if nothing else, that Williams was human. He couldn't do everything right. Siebert did all that was expected of him, and more. Romo was just a gamble who didn't pay off. He went to Chicago a year later in the Josephson deal.

By dealing off Harrelson, the Red Sox hurt themselves in other ways. Although no hot shot at either position, Harrelson could play both first base and right field. In a sense, the progression of trades to correct weaknesses started with him. Since Tony Conigliaro hadn't yet recovered, the Red Sox needed help in right. With George Scott playing third, they needed help at first. They gave up on Scott, who wasn't hitting, and sent him to Milwaukee in the multiple trade after the 1971 season. That left a permanent hole at first, which was why the Red Sox traded Lyle for Cater in early 1972.

The rest of the infield was radically changed between 1967 and 1972. The club's faith in Doug Griffin as a second baseman made Andrews expendable. They traded him to the White Sox with Luis Alvarado for an old, but experienced and still good shortstop, Luis Aparicio.

All these machinations left O'Connell wide open for criticism of practically all his trades after 1967. But they were all necessary, for various reasons. My personal conviction is that, with all their weaknesses, the Red Sox might still have repeated in 1968 if Lonborg had remained healthy. He was not only a winner, but, like Yastrzemski, an inspiration to other pitchers. If he had continued to be a winner, he would have continued as an inspiration. Dick Williams needed no pennant to find self-confidence; he was oozing with it. But with Lonborg he could have added another pennant in 1968.

None of the deals the Red Sox made after 1967 cost them pennants, but I remember an earlier trade which very well might have. In 1952, while there was still plenty of 1946 strength left, they made an incomprehensible deal with Detroit, which dropped any pennant hopes down the drain. The deal was made in early June, three days before the Red Sox opened a five-game series with the Tigers at Fenway Park.

They gave Detroit Johnny Pesky, Walt Dropo, Fred Hatfield, Don Lenhardt, and Bill Wight in return for George Kell, Hoot Evers, Johnny Lipon, and Dizzy Trout. Kell was an all-star third baseman and a solid hitter, but Evers and Trout had seen better days, and Lipon was a second-string shortstop.

Pesky, although not in Kell's class (nobody was in those years), was still a fine third baseman and a good spray hitter. Dropo, despite his 1951 sophomore slump, was showing signs of returning to his 1950 form. At the time of the trade he led the Red Sox in RBIs. With Williams in the service, Lenhardt led the club in homers. Wight was as good a pitcher as Trout at that time, and Hatfield, an outstanding clutch hitter, a better utility infielder than Lipon.

New England's reaction to the trade was epitomized by this anonymous gag: "The Red Sox were leading the league. They had to do something."

One of baseball's oldest bromides is that the best trades are those that result in pennants for both teams. The 1952 deal with Detroit did just the opposite. The Red Sox finished sixth, and the Tigers in the cellar. Neither could have done much worse.

Frank Lane, one of the most active wheeler-dealering general managers in baseball history, always worked on the theory that if you can't win, trade. You have nothing to lose and you're giving your customers new faces. Lane, who once traded managers with Detroit when he was running the Cleveland club, had dealt off hundreds of ballplayers, but he rarely did business with the Red Sox when Joe Cronin was GM.

"Cronin is scared to death that I'll get the best of him," Lane once told me. "The Jimmy Piersall deal is the only big one I can remember when he was there, but I made that one with Yawkey."

I never did get the story of that deal straight. The only thing I know is that Yawkey, for reasons of his own, was determined to get rid of Piersall. Perhaps Piersall had done something that rubbed him the wrong way, but to this day Jimmy has no idea what it was. In any event, Lane was one of his greatest admirers and had made some unsuccessful attempts to get him.

There's no doubt that the deal was made between Lane and Yawkey when the two ran into each other in a hotel lobby during the winter meetings of 1958. And there's no doubt that the first name Lane mentioned to Yawkey was Gary Geiger, at that time a completely unknown outfielder.

The first story I heard was that Yawkey and Lane shook hands on that deal—Piersall for Geiger. According to that version, while the deal was being made, Cronin and Mike Higgins were negotiating with another club for a deal involving Piersall. When Cronin heard Yawkey had already dealt Piersall off, he presumably went to Lane and raked him over the coals for taking advantage of Yawkey. Lane then threw Vic Wertz into the deal, and Cronin was satisfied.

But that's not the way Lane recently told it to Harold Kaese of the Boston *Globe*. Lane says he mentioned Geiger to Yawkey, but Yawkey wouldn't bite because he had never heard of Geiger. When Lane added Vic Wertz, Yawkey shook hands on it. Just then, Cronin and Higgins walked into Yawkey's suite and when Yawkey told them about the trade, they advised him to sleep on it. But the trade was made, and it turned out well for both clubs, although neither won a pennant because of it.

Another American League general manager later told me he wasn't surprised that it took Yawkey to complete the deal.

"You can't do business with the Red Sox," he said. "Cronin wants to sleep on everything. You think things are all settled and he starts backing out. Unless he's absolutely certain he will get the best of it, he won't deal. I gave up on him years ago."

The club this man represented had indeed done very little trading with the Red Sox during Cronin's tenure. Except for isolated trades, usually man-for-man, few clubs did after the big 1952 deal with Detroit. Maybe that one made Cronin cautious. Or maybe he was spoiled by the ease with which he originally could make deals with Yawkey's money. One thing is sure: neither he nor Higgins were good traders after money stopped being the big factor.

CHAPTER 11

Country Club Capers

No other big league team has been more accurately described as a country club than the Red Sox. While teams with less ability won pennants by keeping their noses to the grindstone, there were always some Red Sox players who didn't even know there was a grindstone. The avowed determination of their managers to maintain a hard line on training rules usually crumbled into hopeless resignation. No matter how determined, no manager, up to Dick Williams in 1967, succeeded in curbing the monumental imbibing, bed-hopping, and general shenanigans of the Red Sox players.

Obviously, not every player was a playboy, but since the playboys couldn't be publicly identified, everybody was tarred with the same brush. Every Red Sox team had its share of decent, reasonable, hard-working, dedicated athletes who stuck to their knitting, kept the training faith, worked their brains out, and always showed up at the park ready to play ball.

Their attitude toward their sinning teammates was much

the same as most of the managers'—resignation. Knowing there was nothing they could do to pound sense into empty heads, they shrugged their shoulders and hoped that last night's activities wouldn't ruin today's play. There was no point in reporting what they knew to the boss, even if they wanted to; he didn't have to be told.

Some of the less noble athletes got away with murder and still managed to play good ball—for a few years. The antics of a twenty-two-year-old rarely catch up with him until he's about thirty. Some can even burn the candle at both ends and last indefinitely. Witness the great Yankee teams, many of whose stars were as effective off the ball field as on. Maybe they were fundamentally better ballplayers than the Red Sox. Or had more endurance and a greater will to win. Or took more nights off from the bright lights, or had strong enough feet to kick the lady friend out of bed in time to get a good night's sleep. It was Joe McCarthy, when he was manager of the Yankees, who observed, "A broad is as good in bed before midnight as after, so don't let her interfere with your rest."

Besides the sinners with a predilection for liquor and women, the Red Sox seem to have had more than their share of characters—malingerers, screwballs, flakes, team-jumpers, simple-minded children of nature, bellyachers, loafers, creatures of mood, and genuine comedians. No matter how infuriating the antics of these grown men, it was impossible to take all their training infractions seriously, if only because of the ridiculous circumstances.

Who could fault a Gene Conley-Pumpsie Green combination that broke up for a day over whether or not to go to Israel to teach baseball? Or who took an old-fashioned buggy and rode it around town, with one pulling and the other in the driver's seat with a fake whip? Who, for that matter, could fault anyone for providing laughs? Sometimes only a sense of humor kept the brass from going nuts over the capers of their ballplayers. Often, too, the most serious circumstances were transformed into belly laughs.

There was, for example, Jackie Jensen's hypnotist and Frank Malzone's bum leg. Jensen, a serious athlete and a devoted husband and father, who led the American League three times in RBIs, had a horror of flying. After trying everything else without success, he got his own personal hypnotist, who managed to help him for a while.

Enthusiastic about the powers of hypnosis, Jensen urged his teammates to use his miracle man for their problems. Most declined with thanks. But when Malzone got discouraged over a leg muscle injury that was slow responding to treatment, he finally agreed to let the hypnotist go to work on him.

The great experiment took place in the trainer's quarters off the locker room about two hours before a ball game. Everyone on the premises crowded into the room to watch. Malzone limped to a training table, climbed up, lay flat on his back, and with an obviously jaundiced eye, looked up at the hypnotist.

"You must cooperate," the man said. "That is essential. Cooperate. Trust me. Put yourself in my hands. Relax. Cooperate. I will help you, but only if you cooperate."

"OK," said Malzone. "I'm cooperating."

The hypnotist pulled out a shiny coin and moved it gently back and forth in front of Malzone's face.

"You are getting drowsy . . . your eyes are closing . . .

you are thoroughly relaxed . . . you are going to sleep . . . sleep . . . sleep . . ."

The soft voice droned on endlessly, repeating the words while the observers watched, half fascinated, half skeptical. Pretty soon, Malzone's eyelids grew heavy, and at last his eyes closed. The hypnotist continued to croon softly, his voice sugary, the words never changing. This went on for perhaps twenty minutes.

Then, in the same soothing voice: "When you wake up you will get off the table and lean all your weight on your foot and it won't hurt . . . remember . . . it won't hurt . . . won't hurt . . ."

Now the only sounds in the room were the hypnotist's voice and Malzone's regular breathing. The words were repeated over and over until at last, the man said, "Now you will wake up when I count three . . . when I count three . . . three . . . three . . . and when you put your weight on your foot, it won't hurt . . ." Over and over, the hypnotist repeated these words. Then, his voice rising, he counted.

"One—two—*THREE!*"

Malzone stirred, his eyes fluttered, and he woke up. While everyone watched, completely captivated, he sat up, letting his legs swing over the table. After a short pause, he leaned on his hands and jumped off, landing hard on both feet.

"CHEE-ZUS KEE-RIST!" he howled.

As he scrambled back onto the table, holding his leg in anguish, the hypnotist turned away and muttered, "Wouldn't cooperate."

Apparently Jensen wouldn't either, after a while. His fear

of flying returned and actually drove him out of baseball.

There was Frank Sullivan and his toy racing cars. Once while the team was on the road during Mike Higgins's management, Sullivan ran across an electric racing game in a department store. It consisted of several sets of tracks, one for each car, with the cars operated by individual switches. The equipment was so heavy that Sullivan needed a special case for it.

If nothing else, the racing game kept the players in the hotel. Everywhere the ball club went, the first thing Sullivan did was set up the tracks, let the boys draw lots for cars, and when there was time, have a race or two before going to the ball park. Whether a man had a car or not, everyone bet, and pretty soon Sullivan had gambling games going that sometimes lasted to dawn.

The game became so popular that one set wasn't enough. When Sullivan bought two or three more, he needed help carrying them around. Almost everyone on the ball club loved these races. Even the serious athletes often dropped by to watch and sometimes bet for an hour or two. It may well have been the only time since World War II when every player could be located on the road, day or night.

The electric car craze lasted almost a whole season, with the men on the team more wrapped up in auto races than pennant races. Ball games were secondary, to be gotten over with so the boys could get back to the races. Some of the guys couldn't even remember whether they won or lost at the ball park. All they could think of was Sullivan's wonderful little contraptions.

The races palled at last, and Sullivan somewhat sadly left them in hotel rooms along the way. The hotel people

themselves sighed with relief. No longer would mainte-
nance men have to move furniture back where it belonged.
No longer were neighboring guests kept up most of the
night as ballplayers yelled encouragement to favorites—
"Red, come on red! Blue! Get 'im, blue! Go—go, green!"

With the passing of the auto races, conventional sports
like lifting elbows and chasing broads returned to their
rightful places in the Red Sox entertainment picture.

"So help me," a coach told me one day, "it's better this
way. The guys might be out late, but at least they don't
stay up all night. All they could do was bet and sleep. Now
they think about baseball once in a while."

Before and after the auto races, the best description of
the team's road habits came from a ballplayer who said, "If
at four in the morning a hydrogen bomb were dropped on
our hotel there would always be enough guys out so we
could put a whole team on the field the next night."

Sullivan's buddy was Sammy White, one of the best
catchers the Red Sox ever had, but a flake in the true Sullivan mold. White had light blue eyes which sometimes
seemed to stop working when something came into his
head. Interviewing him was an adventure in confusion.
Sometimes you had to repeat a question half a dozen times
before he snapped out of whatever spell he had put himself
into. Then he would fix those hypnotic eyes on you and
say, "Were you talking to me?"

His specialty behind the plate was handling a catcher's
most difficult chances—low breaking balls that hit the dirt
and skid crazily off. Many fans think the most common
wild pitch is one that goes high over everyone's head or
well off to one side. But any catcher will testify that there's

nothing tougher to handle or thrown more often than a low, skidding pitch.

White stopped them so consistently that Casey Stengel, when he managed the Yankees, said, "The guy's like a snake."

White's career ended abruptly when the Red Sox traded him to Cleveland; he refused to go. Instead, with the backing of a wealthy friend, he opened a bowling alley in the Boston suburb of Brighton with his name inscribed in lights on the roof. The place has since grown to a general entertainment facility and White is long gone, but his name still flashes across the horizon from that roof.

The first time Curt Gowdy went to Honolulu to broadcast the Hula Bowl football game, he had a phone call at his hotel room. Before going to NBC Gowdy had been the Red Sox announcer for years. The voice on the other end sounded vaguely familiar, but Gowdy couldn't quite place it.

After a minute or so, he finally said, "For the love of Mike, who is this?"

"Sammy White."

"Sammy! What the hell are you doing in Honolulu?"

"I'm not in Honolulu," White said. "I'm not even in Oahu. Sully and me are living on another island."

"What are you doing?" Gowdy asked.

"We're professional beachcombers," White said.

One Red Sox star, who shall remain nameless, had a remarkable capacity for beer. When he was with the ball club, there were two hotels (both since sold for college dormitories) in Boston's Kenmore Square, on opposite sides of Commonwealth Avenue: the Kenmore and the

Myles Standish. Each hotel had at least two bars, which the player used to capacity. He would have two beers in one bar, cross the street and have a couple in another, and continue to go back and forth until closing time. In this way, he drank as much as he wanted, but nobody ever saw him have more than two at a time.

One night he had a late date, who met him in a room at the Myles Standish. To celebrate the occasion, he bought a fifth of bourbon, which he and his girl worked on while resting from other activities. Finally, they fell asleep, with a lighted cigar in the player's hand and the bourbon on the bureau. The next thing they knew, firemen were pounding on the door, and the whole room was in smoke. They were lucky to get out with their lives.

The following day, the caption under a newspaper picture of the room read: "On it [the bureau] may be seen a bottle of Joe Shmo's favorite hair tonic."

Joe Shmo was as bald as an egg.

I once asked one of the most renowned Don Juans on the team if his conscience ever bothered him. I'm no prude, but I had seen the guy bid tender farewells to his lovely wife and children, then on the same night I ran into him with another lovely in a drinking joint on the road.

"Why should my conscience bother me?" he retorted. "I never cheat in Boston."

One of Higgins's managerial successors had a player who was enjoying a marvelous season, but at night on the road he was rarely without a bottle under one arm and a girl under the other. In the locker room, he would boom in stentorian tones play-by-play accounts of his most recent exploits. When Joe Cronin had managed the club, he got rid of guys like that fast, with the explanation, "He was a bad influence on young players."

Cronin never had a player who was a worse influence on young players than this bird, who soon began getting the younger players to join him in the fun. At one point in that season, half a dozen players would come rolling into the locker room after a night on the town with their leader, bleary-eyed with hangovers or exhausted from their fun and games. Since they weren't having as great a season as the man leading them astray, they were pretty consistently fined, until they saw the light and looked elsewhere for entertainment. But the captain of this roving wolf pack was doing so well on the field that he even got away with walking in on the manager before a game and telling him he couldn't play.

"Worn out," he would say. Or, "Hung over."

And the manager, grateful for the miracles performed by this superman when the club was having a bad year, promised not to use him, so he could get his rest—during the ball game.

That same year a veteran utility man won several hundred dollars from another player in a gin rummy game in the locker room. After pocketing the money he said, "Nobody on a big-league ball club has a right to win or lose this much in a locker room card game. If I were the manager it would cost us each a thousand."

He wasn't the manager then, but when he later became manager, one of the first things he did was ban high-stake card games on pain of heavy fines. He was also death on hangovers and kiss-and-tell boudoir specialists. This was Dick Williams.

Most managers know which players are sinners and which are saints, but don't fine the sinners until they are sure of their guilt. Rex Sox managers often not only had proof of misbehavior but actually caught men arriving at their hotel long after curfew, yet they imposed few penalties, as far as I could discover. Either they succeeded in keeping the penalties secret or were unable to make them stick because of pressure from the front office. If the latter was true, as it might well have been, I suppose disgusted managers just threw in the towel.

One of the most notorious drunks the Red Sox ever had was a young ballplayer with such great potential that five other clubs gave him chances at different times. The only manager who could control him at all was the late Chuck Dressen, when he ran the Washington Senators (now the Minnesota Twins).

One time in Boston after curfew, Dressen gave the elevator man at the Kenmore Hotel a baseball and told him to get the signatures of every ballplayer who came in from the lobby during the night. Dressen knew the former Red Sox player was the only man out because he had personally run a post-curfew bed check. The next morning the elevator man give him back the baseball without a name on it, so Dressen left word for the errant player to phone him.

The call came at about ten-thirty in the morning.

"Just came down from my room and found a message to call you, Chuck," the ballplayer said.

"It'll cost you five hundred," said Dressen.

"For one night out in Boston?"

"And three in Cleveland and three in Detroit and two in Chicago," Dressen said.

He was the only manager who could keep the guy off the bottle two nights back to back.

"But not any more than that," Dressen told me later at his home in Bel Air, California, "The poor guy was an alcoholic—no doubt about it. I've often thought he would have done a lot better if the Red Sox had slapped heavy fines on him right from the start. At least they might have kept him sober during the season. I tell you, that guy could have made the Hall of Fame. He had more natural talent than anyone I ever saw, and he left it all in barrooms."

Dressen stared at the haze of smog over Los Angeles far below, then said, "That's the trouble with the Red Sox. They get these absolutely marvelous young ballplayers and then spoil the hell out of them."

The Red Sox never penalized errant kids much. One time, two promising rookies were slightly hurt in an automobile accident in Scottsdale. Only the front office seemed to feel sorry for them. Since neither was seriously injured, everyone else wondered why they weren't fined a bundle. The accident occurred at two-thirty in the morning.

One budding young Red Sox star, apparently doing the first serious drinking of his life at a party in New York, got deathly sick in the locker room the next day. When he admitted to the manager that he was hung over, all it cost him was a modest fine and a lecture on the evils of alcohol. Since the manager was a pretty good drinker himself, even that didn't come from the heart.

Ellis Kinder was one of the rare characters who could drink enormous amounts of liquor—which he did openly, in front of managers and everyone else—and still pitch amazingly good ball. One night on a train between Chicago and

Cleveland, he was sitting in the club car with two or three others in the Red Sox party, including Lou Boudreau, who was then the manager. Every time Kinder ordered a bourbon, Boudreau, a teetotaler, had a coke.

At about quarter to twelve, Boudreau yawned, stood up, and said pointedly, "Nearly curfew. I'm going to bed."

"Go ahead, Skip," said Kinder. "I think I'll stay up a while."

Nobody knew how long Kinder stayed up, but he had to be carried off the train and pushed across the station in a wheel chair the next morning, a murderously hot day. At 7:00 A.M. it was already 96 degrees, and the Red Sox had a 1:30 P.M. doubleheader scheduled with the Indians that afternoon.

Kinder's keepers got him into bed, then got him out again after about four hours' sleep. He needed help getting to the ball park, into his uniform, and finally to the bullpen, where, in the 103-degree heat, he promptly went to sleep.

At that point in his career, Kinder was probably the best relief pitcher in the American League, and Boudreau knew that on a day like that no starting pitcher could get through a game without help. Sure enough, the starter wilted in the sixth inning, and Boudreau told the bullpen to warm Kinder up.

"He's asleep," the bullpen coach said.

"I don't care if he's dead," Boudreau snapped. "Get him up."

After stalling about ten minutes by making a couple of slow pilgrimages to the field, Boudreau signaled the bullpen to send Kinder in. Without even a cart to ride in,

Kinder shuffled to the mound, took the ball from Boudreau without a word, threw a few warmup pitches, and went to work.

He got out of the sixth-inning mess the starting pitcher had left, then held the Indians hitless in the seventh, eighth, and ninth to save the ball game.

In the locker room between games, Boudreau said, "Ellie, how you did that after last night I'll never know. Take the rest of the day off."

"Oh, what the hell, Skip," Kinder said. "I'll stick around. Might come in handy later."

He was asleep in the bullpen before the second game began. The starting pitcher made it through the seventh inning that time, so Boudreau phoned the bullpen and said, "What about Ellie?"

"You want me to let him sleep?" the coach asked.

"Just wake him and see if he feels like working," Boudreau said.

Kinder indeed felt like working. He pitched two more hitless innings for his second save of the day. It was the greatest exhibition of hung-over pitching since Grover Cleveland Alexander stopped the Yankees in the seventh game to give the Cardinals the 1926 World Series.

Kinder was the most casual good ballplayer I ever saw. Nothing bothered him. He had once been a railroad worker and cab driver in Jackson, Tennessee, pitching semi-pro ball on Sundays. That's where a St. Louis Browns scout saw him. After coming to the Red Sox in the 1947 deal that cost Yawkey about half a million dollars, he hit it big financially, got a divorce, married a Boston girl, and drove Cadillacs for years.

After his playing career was over, he left town as casually as he had come in, divorced his Boston wife, and went back to Tennessee. He lived with his first wife and her second husband, and within a year or two was back driving a cab in Jackson. He died in the late sixties, but I'm sure if he had his life to live over again he wouldn't change a thing.

Gene Conley didn't need Pumpsie Green to be funny. One day he showed up at Fenway Park after a two-day absence and said to Manager Mike Higgins, "Sorry, Mike. There was sickness in my family."

"Who was sick?" Higgins asked.

"Me," Conley said.

I first met Conley in 1952 in Richland, Washington, when he was a Braves rookie. Bill Sullivan, then the Braves press agent and now president of the New England Patriots football team, was acting as shepherd for a flock of journalists visiting Braves rookies at their homes around the country.

Conley had reached his full height of six-foot-eight then, a lean kid with a twisted grin and a casual, relaxed sense of wry humor. He was a medium good pitcher but never a standout and wandered from team to team in the majors until he landed with the Red Sox. Better at basketball than baseball, he signed a contract with the Boston Celtics while still pitching, much to the chagrin of the Red Sox brass.

"What's the difference?" Conley told his baseball bosses, when they objected to his dual role, fearing he'd get hurt in the rugged National Basketball Association. "I'm too young to die, too old to last, too big to get pushed around, and too dumb to get hurt."

Others have tried two pro sports at once, but only Conley kept at it for any length of time. As backup man for Bill Russell at center, he helped the Celtics win several championships, while always standing ready to pitch when the Red Sox needed him.

One of the funniest characters around the locker room in the early sixties was also one of the most infuriating. Dick Stuart, a muscle-bound first baseman, lost two games with his horrible fielding for every one he won with his batting. A right-handed power hitter, he should have been perfect for Fenway Park, if hitting were all he had to do. He actually averaged about 35 homers and 100 RBIs a year, but the price the team paid was much too high.

Besides being a demoralizing influence in the field, Stuart was just as demoralizing in the locker room. Without regard for whether the Red Sox won or lost, he thought only of his own hitting. They could drop a 10–3 ball game, but Stuart would be happy if the three runs included a homer or two by him.

He made life particularly miserable for Manager Johnny Pesky. Stuart rode Pesky unmercifully and undoubtedly had a good deal to do with his eventually losing the job. Pesky had been a slap hitter with few home runs during a long and outstanding career. Stuart was strictly a slugger who looked down his nose at everyone who wasn't.

In those dark ages of their history, the ball club needed a Dick Stuart like a hole in the head. The next manager, Billy Herman, who had been a coach under Pesky, did little besides getting rid of Stuart. He got the front office to trade Stuart to the Phillies for Dennis Bennett, the sore-armed pitcher.

That summer, 1965, the Red Sox had a horrible year, finishing ninth. The following January, the Boston baseball writers invited Stuart, who lived in Connecticut, to speak at their annual banquet. The opening line of Stuart's talk, delivered to more than a thousand Boston fans, was too memorable to be lost.

Looking down the head table at Herman, Stuart said, "Well, Billy, I hope you're having a good winter. You sure had a horseshit summer."

For years Stuart was the major-league arm wrestling champion, an achievement he bragged about as much as his home runs. I don't think anyone ever beat him, but Ken Harrelson might have if they had ever met in mortal combat.

Harrelson was one of the strongest men ever to play big-league ball. He was a Savannah boy, who grew up with an abiding love for courtesy, mother, sports, gambling, pool, and any chicks who happened to be handy. A most amazing character. Harrelson would bet on anything. More than once he won meal money by arm wrestling or playing pool, at which he was an expert. He could hustle if necessary, but was so good he usually didn't have to.

A natural athlete, Harrelson was one of the best schoolboy football quarterbacks in the south, but he gave up the game for fear an injury would ruin him for baseball, which he really loved. He was also an outstanding basketball player, automobile racer, and golfer. A week or so after he started playing golf, at age sixteen, he broke a hundred, and soon was consistently in the seventies. Most of the time he was in the majors he held the title of baseball's golf champion.

Money went through his hands like quicksilver. When owner Charles Finley of the Kansas City A's fired him in a pique of anger, Harrelson already owed him several thousand dollars for loans against future salary. By cutting him loose in 1967, in the prime of his baseball career, Finley did him a great favor, since he was then a free agent who could sell himself to the highest bidder.

The Red Sox got him for something like $75,000, enabling him to square himself with Finley and indulge his passion for elegant clothes. Harrelson was the fashion plate of the sports world, spending as much as ten thousand a year on clothes.

He and Boston took to each other like ham and eggs. He loved the town, the Red Sox, Fenway Park, and his fantastic apartment in which a round bed with a black silk bedspread, took up almost every square inch of the bedroom. Harrelson even loved his attorney, Bob Woolf, as long as he lasted. Woolf, a highly successful representative of sports stars, loved Harrelson dearly, as did everyone who knew him, but just couldn't keep up with the Hawk's expensive tastes. After two years of watching Harrelson ignore his financial advice, Woolf finally quit.

When the Red Sox traded Harrelson to Cleveland in April of 1969, after he had had a fabulous season in 1968, the Hawk was so hurt he quit baseball altogether. That lasted just long enough for Woolf to escort him to New York, where the two went into a huddle with Baseball Commissioner Bowie Kuhn, Dick O'Connell of the Red Sox, and Gabe Paul, president of the Indians. They had to pry loose a chunk of Fort Knox to get Harrelson to go to Cleveland.

With all his carefree attitude toward life, Harrelson was a serious, conscientious ballplayer, deeply concerned with the ball club.

"He was more of a leader than most people gave him credit for," I was told by a former Red Sox teammate who has since been traded himself. "He was always sitting around talking about how we looked, what we needed, why we should keep going for the pennant and all that. I don't care what he did off the field, but he was all baseball once he got to the park. He hustled all the time, worked hard, took extra hours of batting practice. He was interested, enthusiastic, and confident, and could infect the rest of the guys with that confidence. People accepted him as just a mod playboy, but he was far more than that in a baseball uniform. Everybody liked him and everybody listened to him. Sometimes we'd sit around in a bar and Hawk would say, 'Our baserunning is terrible. We've got to get on those guys. You can win ball games with good baserunning. Let's get better on the bases.' Call me crazy if you want to, but that guy would make somebody a great manager."

The Hawk was never happy in Cleveland. He retired from baseball, this time for real, in the middle of the 1971 season, to become a professional golfer. At present, he's back in Savannah, polishing up his game. He qualified for the 1972 British Open, but failed to survive the cut after he got there. Despite all his sidelines and other interests, his powers of concentration are so great that he's likely to fool everyone and become a real star on the demanding pro golf circuit.

Another memorable character on the Red Sox list was Jimmy Piersall. Piersall was one of the first persons in the public eye to admit to mental illness and to having had shock treatments in an institution as a cure. Long after his recovery, his sharp sense of humor helped keep him on an even keel and convulsed his friends.

One opening day in Washington, when President Eisenhower threw out the first ball, Piersall ignored the other players going after the ball for the President's signature. Instead, he walked up to Eisenhower's box, held out another ball, and said, "Mr. President, while those idiots are scrambling for that ball, would you mind autographing this one for me?" With a big grin, the President obliged.

After Piersall was traded to Cleveland, he kept getting into jams with both General Manager Frank Lane and Manager Joe Gordon. In the spring of 1960, Jimmy had a wire from his friend John F. Kennedy, then a senator. It read: "Dear Jimmy: Do you have any ideas that might be helpful in the Ohio campaign? Jack Kennedy."

Piersall's reply was a minor classic, which Kennedy got a big kick out of. It read: "Dear Jack: I'm having big troubles with Lane and Gordon. Please don't bother me with your little ones."

At one World Series, he had a lock on all the Yankee scoops. Covering the Series for the Boston *Globe*, he was the only baseball writer in history for whom the players lined up to be interviewed. Everyone from Mickey Mantle down stood in the line, while Piersall scribbled priceless remarks that the Yankee players had saved for him.

While Piersall was still with the Red Sox, they once picked up Mickey Owen as a spare catcher. Owen had won everlasting notoriety by dropping a third strike that cost the Brooklyn Dodgers one of the 1941 World Series games against the Yankees.

Later, Owen became a manager in the North Carolina State League, where he was in constant hassles with umpires and opposing ballplayers. One day, while the Red Sox were barnstorming through North Carolina, Owen told of the time he got into a fight so vicious that he bit off an adversary's ear. As Owen told the story, Piersall's big brown eyes became wider and wider. When he finished, Jimmy shook his head and said, "And they called *me* crazy."

Piersall, Jackie Jensen, and Ted Williams formed one of baseball's best outfields. A magician with a glove, Piersall specialized in making fantastic catches other outfielders could never get near. All over the American League there were walls pockmarked with spike holes made by this most amazing outfielder.

Jensen was a better than average fielder and a great clutch hitter, at his best with men on base. He was also a great football running back. To this day, he is the only athlete ever to play in the Rose Bowl (for California) and the World Series (for the Yankees, with whom he broke into the majors).

And Ted Williams was, of course, Ted Williams. Each had his own personality quirks. Even after recovering from his mental illness, Piersall, an intense ballplayer who considered every umpire his natural enemy, was their scourge for years. He squawked at so many calls that some umpires got into the habit of thumbing him out of games before he even got going. Once, all three base umpires came at him as he stood with his bat in his hand, arguing with the plate umpire over a called strike.

He stopped when he saw the other three approaching, dropped his bat, grinned, and said, "What the hell's the matter with you guys? You look like keepers chasing a lunatic. You'd all look better in white coats."

That broke the tension. Everybody laughed and moved back to their regular posts.

Jensen's thing, of course, was his fear of flying. It was shared by Gary Geiger, the outfielder who came to the Red Sox in the Piersall deal. Later, other Red Sox, notably Carl Yastrzemski, developed the same fear. They all learned to live with it after Jensen left the ball club, but as long as he wore a Red Sox uniform, at least three or four men on the team refused to fly except when there was no other way of reaching a destination on time.

Although Williams was always the dominant character on the ball club, he was sometimes overshadowed by Jensen and Piersall when they were his outfield mates. The others had their special problems, but Williams's problems were all of his own making.

For some reason, the Red Sox lost more men who quit while they were still fine players than any other team in the majors. Flying drove Jensen out. A trade drove Sammy White out. Manager Lou Boudreau's failure to play him drove Dom DiMaggio out. Dick Williams's failure to play *him* drove Joe Azcue out, although he came back after the Red Sox traded him. A trade drove Hawk Harrelson out, although a sweetened pot brought him back. Sore arms drove more than a dozen pitchers out, most notably Tex Hughson, Mickey Harris, Boo Ferriss, Dave Morehead, and Jose Santiago. Back problems drove out stars like George Kell, Bobby Doerr, and Haywood Sullivan. Sins of the flesh and the palate drove out dozens of guys who might otherwise have become stars.

Once Manager Billy Herman, trying to trap some of his worst offenders, pulled a sudden bed check on the whole club after curfew in Washington. Somebody got wind of it and tipped off all the bad boys, every one of whom was tucked neatly into bed—alone—when the check was made. But it happened that six notoriously good boys picked that night to attend a stag party. They were the only fish Herman netted. Disgusted, he threw them all back into the water without penalty.

It is a truism in baseball, as well as other professional sports, that the worst time to pull a bed check is on the last stop before the club goes home. With wives to face, even the most outrageous sinners will usually observe curfew.

Fun is fun, unless it interferes with a man's play on the field. And that was always the trouble with the Red Sox. The managers and front office personnel assumed everyone was ready to play ball, no matter how active a night he had spent.

But everybody wasn't always ready. A clampdown at the right time might have helped. But too many Red Sox managers said, in effect, "Why put juvenile checks on grown men?"

Because too many of the grown men were juveniles, that's why.

CHAPTER 12

Forgive and Forget

Ted Williams retired from baseball at the end of the 1960 season. Taking his place in left field the following year was another superstar, who looked the part almost from the beginning. From 1961 on, Carl Yastrzemski was the dominant figure on the Red Sox.

Like Williams, Yastrzemski was a left-handed batter with a dream swing. Although he lacked Williams's height, strength, and power, he had all the ingredients of a star. In a sense, he was a product of Williams, who was his batting coach for several years in spring training. Williams agreed with every other competent observer who predicted great things for the twenty-two-year-old rookie.

Yastrzemski, older of two sons of a potato farmer in the small, predominantly Polish town of Bridghampton, thirty miles from the tip of Long Island, had baseball in his blood. His father, Carl, Sr., was manager of a semi-pro baseball team, on which the two played together for several years. When he signed a Red Sox contract for a bonus that ran into six figures, Yastrzemski was already being groomed as Williams's replacement.

He joined the team under pressure, and in the years since, he has survived Boston's unique baseball pressure cooker, which has shriveled more than one good man. The spotlight that once was focused on Williams has been redirected at Yastrzemski.

A three-time American League batting champion and hero of the Impossible Dream season of 1967, Yastrzemski has been maligned by the press, fingered as the villain whenever things went wrong with the club, and been made the victim of as many misunderstandings as Williams.

Unlike Williams, Yastrzemski, who is much more even-tempered, never harbored lengthy personal grudges against either the Boston press or the team's fickle fans. He once vowed never to tip his cap after home runs, but was talked out of it. He sometimes refuses to speak to writers who have gone out of their way to hurt him, but his animosity toward them is never permanent. Where Williams openly talked of his hatred for the press, Yastrzemski generally keeps his own counsel on the subject.

There are other differences between the two Red Sox stars. Williams was brash, loud, and outspoken. Yastrzemski is shy, quiet, and taciturn. Williams had a keen sense of humor; Yastrzemski's is muted, sometimes bitter. Despite his problems with some people, Williams was gregarious and enjoyed close associations with many. Yastrzemski is inclined to be a loner, although he has a very small circle of trusted friends. Williams talked well and fluently. Yastrzemski is capable of doing so, but has been burned so often that he now seldom says what he thinks.

Williams was primarily a slugger, although he made himself into a pretty good outfielder, learned to play the Wall in left field, and had a good arm. Yastrzemski is not primarily a slugger, although he can hit for distance. Other than that, he is a more complete player than Williams. A marvelously well-coordinated athlete, a far better fielder than Williams, Yastrzemski plays the Wall better, has a better arm, runs faster, and has better baseball instincts.

Their leadership qualities are about the same—not very good. Both led more by example than anything else; both were looked up to by teammates, but Williams never could fire up his mates. Yastrzemski did in 1967, the year the Red Sox won the pennant. But he never achieved those heights of leadership again.

In a way, Yastrzemski is a victim of what Williams had been. Williams could take a verbal or journalistic beating better because he had a real desire to strike back and the cleverness to hit where it hurt most. Williams liked the give-and-take of fighting city hall, the press, or anything else that seemed to loom as an obstacle. Yastrzemski will not run away from a fight, but he does not enjoy combat, especially of the verbal variety.

Williams was moody, even when talking. Yastrzemski's moods show in other ways. When he is down, he simply clams up or disappears into an anteroom off the locker room. Like most big-league ballplayers, both had friends all over the circuit. But few of their friends, either in or out of Boston, were baseball people.

Williams came into Boston a loner, too young and too brash to have any close friends on the club. He departed a loner, having outlasted all his old teammates and outgrown all his new ones.

Yastrzemski came into Boston with one very close friend, Chuck Schilling, a second baseman and fellow Long Islander. He always felt that Schilling never got a fair shake from any Red Sox manager for whom he played. Yastrzemski resented Johnny Pesky for not playing Schilling and never quite forgave Billy Herman for trading him. Schilling is now out of baseball, but to this day, Yastrzemski thinks he would have been a star if handled properly.

One of the biggest mistakes made by the Boston press, and apparently believed by many Red Sox fans, is that Yastrzemski runs the ball club from his locker beneath the Fenway Park grandstand. This is absurd. Yastrzemski has now played for five managers. It is generally accepted as fact in Boston baseball circles that he was directly responsible for the firing of three and holds the fate of a fourth in his hands because of a special pipeline to Tom Yawkey's office.

That, too, is absurd. Yastrzemski and Yawkey are close friends, but it is the friendship of an older man for a younger, an admired boss for a valued employee. Yastrzemski barely knew Yawkey his first few years up. Their first close association occurred in 1965 when Yastrzemski suffered a kidney injury which landed him in the hospital for nine days. During that period Yawkey didn't miss a day visiting him. The two whiled away long hours and came to know each other well.

But it was not a friendship of contemporaries, nor did it have any profound effect on their relationship. Yastrzemski was, and continues to be, deeply grateful to Yawkey, both for his concern when he was sick and later for his generosity after the Red Sox won the 1967 pennant.

Because of that pennant and what Yastrzemski has meant

to the Red Sox, I certainly doubt that Yawkey will ever trade him. But, at the same time, neither has Yastrzemski a better pipeline to Tom Yawkey than anyone else on the club.

Today Yastrzemski has a warm but arm's-length relationship with Yawkey. He sees Yawkey only when Yawkey initiates a meeting and talks to Yawkey only when Yawkey calls him. They have never socialized except on the one occasion the whole team socialized with Yawkey, the night the Red Sox clinched the 1967 pennant.

Although Yastrzemski has often been accused of instigating managerial changes, he has had nothing to do with any of them. The first time this accusation popped up was when Johnny Pesky was fired just before the end of the 1964 season. It was no secret that the two disliked each other or that Pesky had accused Yastrzemski of not hustling. But Pesky was fired for two reasons. Hired by Yawkey personally, he was never in the good graces of the general manager, Mike Higgins. Higgins couldn't wait for an excuse to get rid of him. The excuse was the collapse of the team in midseason of Pesky's first year, 1963, when they finished seventh, followed by Pesky's inability to improve the club's position his next year, 1964, when they finished eighth. So Higgins's initial animosity was one reason for Pesky's exit, and Pesky's failure to win was the other.

Yet some New England baseball writers still say Yastrzemski got Pesky fired. And this, more than anything, has kept alive the legend of Yastrzemski's power in the front office.

The same thing happened when Herman was fired in 1966 and when Dick Williams was fired at the end of the

1969 season. In both cases, the press fingered Yastrzemski
as the man who triggered these moves. Ridiculous.

Herman had been a coach for many years before he became manager. In those years he and Yastrzemski spent
many traveling hours playing bridge together. They continued to be good friends until just before Herman was
fired. At that time, Herman accused Yastrzemski of ma-
lingering on the ball field and said he would see that he
was traded. Yastrzemski just denied that he hadn't hustled.
Herman told him that one of the two would be gone by
1967. Yastrzemski's reply was that if Herman stayed, he'd
wish to be traded.

This conversation took place in private while the Red
Sox were in Washington. Nobody knew about it at the
time. And even after Herman was fired, Yastrzemski was
still nervous about being traded. He liked Boston, where
he had been living since 1961, and wanted to stay there.
But he was so worried about being traded that he went to
see Dick O'Connell, the general manager, not Yawkey, for
assurance that he would not be traded.

By then Dick Williams had been named as Herman's
successor. Herman's only hope of getting a new contract
after 1966 was to improve the ninth-place finish of 1965.
Instead, he finished ninth again. That, plus his being a
legacy from the Mike Higgins regime, clinched it. Yastrzemski had no more to do with Herman's firing than
with Pesky's.

When Williams became the manager in 1967, one of his
first moves was to disclose that the team would have no
captain. It was not an actual announcement, but an answer
to a writer's question. The press jumped on it as the be-

ginning of a power struggle in the locker room between
Williams and Yastrzemski, because Yastrzemski had been
captain under Billy Herman. What the press didn't know
was that Yastrzemski never wanted the job, thought the
player representative should handle whatever a captain
might do, and hated having to act as middleman between
ballplayers and manager. Before Dick Williams became
manager of the club, Yastrzemski had already told Dick
O'Connell he didn't want to be captain.

Williams wouldn't have thought about a captain if he
hadn't been asked. He had had no captain at Toronto and
knew the Red Sox had none when he played for them. He
considered captains superfluous.

"With a manager, four or five coaches, and a player representative, who needs a captain?" he said. "You end up
with all chiefs and no Indians."

I doubt if Williams even knew the Red Sox had a captain when he got the job, and if he did I'm sure he didn't
know it was Yastrzemski. If he had thought the subject
would become a hot potato, he probably would have side-
stepped the question.

While the press was having a field day over a situation
that implied friction between the star and the new manager, Yastrzemski was delighted to get rid of the job. In
the beginning, in fact, he had spent several weeks fruit-
lessly trying to get out of it. When Herman asked him to
take it, he refused. Herman then decided the players
should elect a captain. In a closed ballot, they chose Yastrzemski, who found himself doing things he thought
were the manager's responsibility.

As far as Herman was concerned, the less direct contact

he had with the players, the better. With Herman virtually incommunicado, players went to Yastrzemski with all their gripes, which he relayed to Herman. That lasted for about ten days, until Herman decided he didn't want to be bothered. From then on, Yastrzemski did what he could to unravel serious situations and ignored everything else.

The biggest problem was Herman's almost pathological dislike of Rico Petrocelli. Petrocelli is now an established star, who broke Junior Stephens's record for home runs by a shortstop in one season by hitting forty in 1969. But then he was a shy, self-effacing kid with almost no self-confidence. In 1965 and 1966 the only person who could do anything with him was Yastrzemski, his locker neighbor. During those first two years, Yastrzemski continually bolstered his ego, telling him again and again that he was a great shortstop with a great career ahead of him. If Yastrzemski stopped him from quitting once, he stopped him a dozen times.

In both years, Petrocelli had several outside problems which Herman either wouldn't or couldn't understand. Once, Petrocelli left the club in the middle of a game because he had a premonition something was wrong at home. When he got there, his wife was rolling around the kitchen floor in agony, suffering from a painful but not serious stomach ailment. He rushed her to the hospital, where she quickly recovered.

That was one of the few occasions Tom Yawkey asked Yastrzemski to see him in his office. When Yastrzemski arrived, the place was in a turmoil. O'Connell was on the phone trying to locate Petrocelli. Herman was demanding that they trade Petrocelli, insisting, "I've got a shortstop who doesn't want to play ball." Yawkey and his wife were quietly discussing the situation.

"Why would Rico do this?" Yawkey asked Yastrzemski.

"Because something's bothering him," Yastrzemski said. "Rico's a worrier. He worries about making the team. He worries about his ailments—he has several nagging little ones, just bad enough to make it hard for him to play. And he worries about his family—he's always worried about his family."

By then O'Connell had located the Petrocellis in a Peabody hospital, on Boston's North Shore. After talking with Petrocelli O'Connell hung up and explained the situation to the Yawkeys. They thanked Yastrzemski for coming, and he left after having spent no more than ten minutes with them.

A couple of days later, Herman fined Petrocelli a thousand dollars, about one-ninth of his salary. That wouldn't have meant much to Petrocelli today, for he now collects about $75,000 a year, but in 1966 it was a terrible belt. That fine stuck, because leaving in the middle of a game is considered a major infraction of the rules.

Yastrzemski was summoned to Yawkey's office not because he was Yastrzemski, but because he was the team captain. It was one of his final duties in that capacity, and the last straw in his successful fight to get rid of the job.

Yet when Dick Williams announced the Red Sox would have no captain in 1967, the press had a field day discussing a sure "confrontation" between Williams and Yastrzemski. The confrontation amounted to a "Thank you" from Yastrzemski and a "You're welcome" from Williams.

Although Yastrzemski did not like Williams personally,

he greatly admired him as a manager and was as surprised as everyone else on the club when Williams was fired. But the Boston press gave the impression that Williams went because Yastrzemski wanted him to. The writers cited the incident of the captaincy as one of the reasons. Like most of his teammates, Yastrzemski definitely did not want to see Williams leave.

"I was totally disgusted when Williams was fired," an ex-Red Sox player told me. "I'd say seventy-five percent of the club felt the same way. That included Carl. He took some of the rap for it, which was completely unfair."

The same man, talking about Yastrzemski's inadequacies as a leader said, "He's the best all-round baseball player in the American League, but his makeup keeps him from being a leader. After leading us by example in 1967 he was supposed to continue to lead us. But he was superman in '67. Nobody, including Carl himself, could ever repeat the things he did then.

"He's a loner, and loners can't be leaders. After Schilling left, he wasn't close to any other ballplayer for years. His best friend in the locker room was Don Fitzpatrick. [Fitzpatrick, then the equipment manager, now has another job in the organization.] He was sort of father confessor to Rico Petrocelli—he saved Petrocelli's career—but they never saw each other socially. He later did become close to Reggie Smith, and probably still is."

This is true. Yastrzemski and Smith, close for years, are now inseparable. This really started because of the location of their lockers. When Smith first joined the club in 1967, he lockered some distance from Yastrzemski, but was shifted to an adjoining locker two years later. The friendship between both star outfielders is one of the best examples of interracial amity in the big leagues.

It also resulted in one of the most amazing hassles baseball has ever seen, a long-drawn-out battle between Billy Conigliaro on one side and Yastrzemski and Smith on the other, during the summer of 1971. Only Yastrzemski's desire for harmony and Manager Eddie Kasko's firmness kept the incident from dividing the Red Sox team and wrecking any chance of success with its present personnel.

In order to understand how this all happened, it is necessary to understand the Conigliaro family, which has been involved in the problems of the Red Sox since Tony, the elder, joined the club in 1964 at the age of nineteen.

Despite all the controversy that swirled around his head while he was with the team, Tony was a ballplayer's ballplayer who loved the game and played it to the hilt. From 1964 through 1970, he batted .270, hit 160 homers, and had 492 RBIs. Since he was out the entire 1968 season and the last half of the 1967 campaign, these are amazing figures. At the time he was hurt, he seemed a sure shot for stardom.

Anyone finding fault with Tony Conigliaro as a ballplayer would be splitting hairs, for he was a stickout. His problem was his personality and his inability to accept success gracefully. He was inclined to be surly and had a tendency to act like a child when things went wrong.

There was never a serious problem between him and Yastrzemski. Although they never got together socially, they were congenial on the field. They didn't talk anything but baseball, for they had nothing else in common. Since Conigliaro followed Yastrzemski in the batting order for years, they'd discuss the opposing pitcher, or maybe a relief pitcher. These two were the fat of the Red Sox batting order, and the opposing manager often called in a man from the bullpen when they were due to come up. So they would stand together watching him warm up and trying to anticipate what he would be most likely to throw.

The only time Yastrzemski tried to help Tony or give him advice was when Conigliaro griped about being booed by the fans one day during his rookie season of 1964. The two met at the entrance to the shower room.

"The hell with the fans," Tony said.

"Don't worry about them," Yastrzemski said. "They're paying your salary. You won't gain anything fighting them."

But Conigliaro would have problems with both the public and the press in the years that followed.

Tony's brother, Billy, three years younger, was something else again. A good major-league prospect, he collected a reported bonus of $60,000 when he signed with the Red Sox. Like Tony, Billy was an outfielder and a long-hitting right-handed batter. But he lacked Tony's ability and enthusiasm for baseball.

The brothers, born and brought up on Boston's North Shore, should have been naturals for the Red Sox, as indeed Tony was until he got hurt in 1967. The biggest difference between them was that Tony loved baseball and Billy could take it or leave it alone. When Billy was on his way up to the majors, he played well without Tony because he knew he had to make it to Boston on his own. In his last year in the minors, he played for Eddie Kasko at Louisville, where he was the regular center fielder, batted .298, and had thirteen homers and eighty-one runs batted in. He and Kasko moved up to the Red Sox together in 1970.

That year Billy beat out Joe Lahoud as the fourth out-fielder behind Yastrzemski in left, Smith in center, and Tony Conigliaro in right. Although he didn't like sitting on the bench, Billy accepted the situation because of Tony. They are exceptionally close and, as later events proved, Billy was happier sitting on the bench with Tony as a team-mate than playing regularly with Tony gone.

An introspective youth, Billy lacked Tony's magnetism. Tony had made a tremendous impact on the Boston public. Handsome, outgoing, a star in every sense of the word who made a magnificent comeback in 1969 after his crippling 1967 injury, Tony had almost as much charisma as Yastrzemski. When Billy joined the club in 1970, he was just "the other Conigliaro."

That situation should have changed when Tony was traded to California during the 1970 World Series, for it left the door open for Billy to play regularly. Kasko put him into center field and shifted Reggie Smith to right for two reasons. Billy had done well for Kasko in center at Louisville, and Smith, who has a great arm, could take better advantage of it as a right fielder than as a center fielder.

But what neither Kasko nor anyone else anticipated was the effect of Tony's departure on Billy. Instead of being happy that there was now a place for him in the regular lineup, Billy became a silent, moody loner who missed Tony more than anyone realized. Although he played well at times, he was nowhere near the center fielder in Boston that he had been in Louisville.

Kasko began platooning Billy, a right-handed hitter,

with Lahoud, a left-hander, which only served to further
upset Billy. Normally, his resentment would have been
directed at Lahoud, the man fighting him for the job. Instead, Billy, for reasons best known to himself, directed it
all at Yastrzemski and Smith.

How he convinced himself that the two were responsible
for Tony's having been traded was impossible for anyone
else to understand, but in the course of the 1971 season
everything spilled out. It began with a rhubarb involving
Yastrzemski, Smith and, indirectly, Lahoud and Tony. But
the basic problem was really Billy's animosity toward Yastrzemski and, to a lesser degree, Smith.

The first blowup came in June after a day game against
the Angels at Fenway Park. With Billy in center field, the
Angels scored a run when a fly ball landed in front of him
for a hit. Afterward, several writers asked Yastrzemski,
"Don't you think Billy plays too deep? He should have
caught that ball."

Yastrzemski laughed and said, "Are you crazy? I'm not
going to get involved in anything like that. How a guy
plays center field here—deep or shallow—is a matter of personal preference."

At this point, all the writers except Clif Keane of the
Boston *Globe* left. To Keane, Yastrzemski said, "The few
times I play center field at Fenway Park I play it shallow.
Because I figure a deep ball will either clear the bleacher
fence and I won't be able to touch it, or it will hit the
fence and I'll be able to play the carom. There's a better
center fielder than I am over in the other locker room, Ken
Berry [the Angels' center fielder that day]. He plays deep,
just like Billy. Why don't you go over and talk to him?"

At this point, several other writers, mostly from suburban or out-of-town New England papers, drifted over to Yastrzemski's locker. They got there just in time to hear Yastrzemski say to Keane, "Find out why he plays it deep and maybe he'll give you reasons why Billy does." That was all the writers needed to be convinced Yastrzemski was criticizing Billy.

Between that and a remark by Reggie Smith, the papers blew up the so-called "dissension" in the Red Sox ranks, giving only secondary attention to the result of the ball game. Someone asked Smith, who played center for some years and was now playing right, what he thought about Kasko shaking up the lineup.

"You always shake up the lineup a little when things go well," he said. "Do something. Maybe play Lahoud a few games."

Yastrzemski criticizing Conigliaro. Smith saying Lahoud should be playing, implying that Conigliaro should be benched in his favor. The two best players on the ball club putting the slug on Tony's kid brother. The newspapers were packed with stories on that subject, while the game stories were buried inside. Suddenly Yastrzemski and Smith were the villains and Billy Conigliaro the victim of a conspiracy to get him out of the lineup.

Billy didn't have to see the papers to know what had been said, because the writers went to him for a rebuttal. Hurt and upset, without Tony beside him, Billy, in trying to defend himself, simply made matters worse. But his basic reaction was cold anger, directed almost entirely at Yastrzemski and Smith.

That night, while waiting at the Boston airport for the

plane to Oakland, where they were opening a series the following Tuesday, Billy swept by Yastrzemski and Smith without a word.

"He's mad," Yastrzemski said. "We've got to straighten this out. Let's get together with Billy and Kasko."

Smith agreed, and through Kasko the two arranged a meeting with Billy the next day, Monday, in Kasko's Oakland hotel room. Yastrzemski and Smith walked in together, and Conigliaro joined them a few minutes later.

His speech larded with four-letter words—the first time Yastrzemski had ever heard Kasko swear—the Red Sox manager snapped, "Shut the bleeping door." Then, "I'll tell you one thing—you're all acting like babies. I want you to get whatever the bleep is on your minds off, and I want you to go out of here and act like men the rest of the year." Then, to Billy, "Have you anything to say?"

"No," Conigliaro said.

"Yaz?" said Kasko.

"Yeah," Yastrzemski said. "I'd like to explain to Billy how this whole thing came about."

After he had told his side of the story, Kasko said, "Reggie?"

Smith then explained how he was using the reference to Lahoud as an illustration of a lineup shakeup, rather than a recommendation, and how his words had been taken out of context. He assured Billy there was nothing personal, and that he didn't mean to make it appear that he preferred to see Lahoud in center field.

"Billy?" said Kasko.

Billy then went off on a slightly different tack, but one which the other three could understand. He talked about how tough it had been with Tony gone, how much he depended on Tony, how much Tony used to help him. Next everyone spoke about Tony, to assure Billy they realized how much the trade had shaken him up.

Finally, Kasko said, "I hope this is the end of it." Opening the door, he added, "My door's always open. Anybody got any bleeping gripes I hope he'll have enough guts to come in and talk them out. It's the only way to get things into their proper perspective."

He then asked each of the three if he had any other gripes. After all had said no, Kasko said, "OK. Now get the hell out of here."

The flap soon blew over, and everything was quiet for about a month—until the last Saturday before the All-Star game. In New York, the Red Sox, about three games off the top in the American League East race, lost a game to the Yankees with two out in the ninth when Billy Conigliaro, playing his normally deep center field, let a ball drop in front of him for the hit that meant the game.

Perhaps it was because ten days earlier Tony had retired from baseball when his sight deteriorated again. Perhaps it was because Billy, despite the conference with Kasko, still harbored a deep grudge against Yastrzemski and Smith. Or perhaps it was because a volcano of unhappiness and loneliness for Tony, churning inside Billy, was waiting to explode.

Whatever the reason, when the press ganged up on Billy to get his slant on the fly ball that had dropped in front of him, he lashed out at Yastrzemski and Smith. He blamed them both for Tony's having been traded.

The first Yastrzemski knew about it was when Fred Ci-

ampa of the Boston *Record-American* said to him, "Do you
have any comment?"

"About what?"

"Billy's statement."

"What statement?"

"That you and Reggie were responsible for getting his
brother traded."

"What the hell are you talking about?" Yastrzemski
asked.

"I just spent half an hour with Billy, and that was all we
talked about," Ciampa said. "Are you going to say anything?"

Yastrzemski, completely flabbergasted, stared at the
writer, then said, "No thanks. This is the first I've heard
about it. I'm not getting involved until I get the whole
story."

Don Fitzpatrick, the equipment manager, broke the
news to Smith, who was waiting to go to dinner with Yastrzemski. Smith, more emotional and less capable of hid-
ing his feelings than Yastrzemski, blew his stack. By that
time, Conigliaro had already left for Boston, where a mili-
tary commitment the next day would keep him out of Sunday's game against the Yankees in New York. Most of all,
Smith resented Conigliaro's making his statement, then
leaving before talking directly either to him or Yastrzemski.

"It was like running away while throwing rocks over
your shoulder," Smith said.

Angry as he was, Smith knew he couldn't talk rationally
for publication, and that day he didn't. But after discussing
the situation with Yastrzemski at dinner and sleeping on it

that night, Smith went to the ball park with his mind made up.

"Neither Reggie nor I had said anything," Yastrzemski said, "but the headlines looked as if we had, and the stories were placed as if somebody had committed murder."

But Smith said plenty when he arrived at Yankee Stadium for the Sunday game: Namely, that he thought Billy Conigliaro should be suspended and that he never wanted to play on the same team with him again. This broke open more speculation, including somebody's conclusion that the basic split on the ball club was between Yastrzemski and Smith on the one hand and Rico Petrocelli, George Scott, and Conigliaro on the other.

Petrocelli and Scott were brought into the controversy only because their Fenway lockers adjoined Conigliaro's. Actually, Petrocelli's only reaction was gratitude to Yastrzemski for having helped him in his years of trouble. He stated positively that he would never take sides with anybody against the Red Sox star. At the time, Scott's reaction was neutral. His feelings generally were governed by the way he was going. When he was hitting he loved everybody. When he wasn't, he didn't like anybody.

It was only later in the season that Scott and Conigliaro really started getting friendly. By then, the whole rhubarb had died down. Billy apologized to Yastrzemski and Smith for his accusation at a meeting after the All-Star game in the office of Joseph Tauro, the Conigliaros' attorney. Smith refused to attend the meeting, but Yastrzemski was there, along with both Tony and Billy. Tony personally apologized to Yastrzemski for Billy, and Billy later released for publication a written apology.

But there was no doubt now that Billy's days with the Red Sox were numbered. Both he and Scott, in fact, openly said they'd be happier elsewhere in 1972. So, along with several other players, they were traded to the Milwaukee Brewers as soon as the 1971 season ended.

The somewhat sad aftermath of the whole affair was Billy's own temporary retirement in late June of 1972 at the age of twenty-four. Only a few weeks earlier, when the Brewers were in Boston, Billy had had an excellent series. Before leaving town, however, he left a bad taste in everyone's mouth when, referring to Kasko, he said, "Maybe he'll be fired and that would be nice."

Kasko was more mystified than hurt.

"I don't know why he said that," the manager later told me. "I never felt any animosity toward him and didn't think there was any on his part toward me. He was a good ballplayer and had the ability to become an outstanding one."

As the 1972 season progressed, however, all such personnel problems seemed to fade away in the face of the club's success. Boston was the surprise team of the second half of the season. Under Eddie Kasko's management, they came within half a game of winning the American League East title. This was great for the fans and players, but embarrassing for the front office. Either Kasko was a better manager than anyone had expected or the Red Sox were luckier than anyone had dreamed.

Whatever the situation, there is no doubt but that the men running the club—General Manager Dick O'Connell and Player Personnel Director Haywood Sullivan—wanted to promote Darrell Johnson to Boston as manager. Johnson had done an outstanding job at Louisville, and other big-league teams were already sounding him out as to his availability.

No one needed to remind O'Connell and his top aide what happened the last time the Red Sox had a managerial talent in the minors whom they didn't bring to Boston. Gene Mauch, still considered by his peers the best manager in baseball, left the fold to go to Philadelphia in 1960, and has been conspicuously managing in the majors ever since.

Meanwhile, the Red Sox floundered around with several lesser men before they promoted Dick Williams. After Yawkey fired him in 1969 and hired Kasko for two years, the front office planned to make the change they wanted when the two years were up. But how could they fire Kasko now? He had come within two days of getting Boston into the playoffs. There was no choice but to give him another two-year contract.

This time, however, they made sure that Johnson would remain in the wings. They gave him a major-league salary to continue to run a minor-league club. The minute Kasko falters—if he does—the Red Sox will pull Johnson up to Fenway Park.

If that happens, he won't have to travel far. Because the top Red Sox farm club has been shifted from Louisville to Pawtucket, Rhode Island, it will be a very simple thing for Johnson to visit Boston and watch the Red Sox play.

On one of those trips, he may stay.